Connect2God

Instant Messages from God to Teens

Curt Cloninger

HONOR **HB** BOOKS

Inspiration and Motivation for the Season of Life

COOK COMMUNICATIONS MINISTRIES
Colorado Springs, Colorado • Paris, Ontario
KINGSWAY COMMUNICATIONS LTD
Eastbourne, England

Honor Books® is an imprint of
Cook Communications Ministries, Colorado Springs, Colorado 80918
Cook Communications, Paris, Ontario
Kingsway Communications Ltd, Eastbourne, England

CONNECT2GOD—INSTANT MESSAGES FROM GOD TO TEENS
© 2004 by CURT CLONINGER

First printing, 2004
Printed in the UNITED STATES OF AMERICA
2 3 4 5 6 Printing/Year 08 07 06 05 04

Developed by Bordon Books
Designed by Chris Gilbert, USD DesignWorks, Inc.

ISBN: 1-56292-259-9

Dedication

For my children, Caroline, Jordan, and Robin. I am so proud of y'all. I can't wait to see what God has planned for you. Like the man says in *James and the Giant Peach,* "Marvelous things will happen!"

Introduction

Ever wish God would just tell you what He thinks? Do you wish He would share how He feels about things? In *Connect2God* you can read God's heart through instant message conversations and messages sent from Him to you. Each entry is based on the kinds of things you go through, such as being overwhelmed by homework or feeling like everyone is doing much better than you are. You can learn what God would likely say to you about what you're feeling.

Each message is also based on the Bible, which is where God really says what He means. That's why we have included a scripture with each instant message so you can have the confidence that the message here is what God really would say.

Feeling lonely and wondering if God has anything to say to you about that? Look at the index in the back and find the message from God on loneliness. Read the Bible promise of Jesus that He will always be with you. You'll feel better after you've understood just how much God loves you, even when you feel as if He isn't there. *Connect2God* will help you discover the guidance and assurance you're looking for to help you face life. So, jump right in and *Connect2God.*

Curt Cloninger

Come Boldly

LOGON>>

<TEEN> Lord, I don't really feel like I should even be talking to you.

<GOD> Why?

<TEEN> Because you are so perfect and good, and I'm not really like that.

<GOD> It's not about how good you are. It's about how much I love you. I seriously want to hang out with you. You are on my VIP guest list. So don't be shy.

<TEEN> You really want me to bother you all the time?

<GOD> It's no bother! It's a pleasure.

Let us have confidence, then, and approach
God's throne, where there is grace.
There we will receive mercy and
find grace to help us just when we need it.

h e b r e w s . 4 : 1 6 . t e v

I want you to come boldly to Me with confidence and trust. It's true that I am the God of the whole universe, but you don't need to be afraid of Me. Even if you have done wrong, there's nothing you can tell Me that will make Me love you less. I am a God of mercy and grace. If you can't bring your wrongs to Me and confess them, then how will you ever get rid of them? Goodness and forgiveness start with Me, and I can't wait to give them to you.

Think of Me as your father. What if your father were the President of the United States? The reporters, ambassadors, and Secret Service agents would have to wait patiently outside his office, but you could go straight in and see him, because he's your dad. It's the same way with Me. I'm never too busy for you. I love you so much. I'm looking forward to knowing you better.

Your loving Father,
God

Talk It Out with God

Stuck
in a Rut

LOGON>>

<TEEN> Jesus, I go to class, come home, do my homework, and start all over again. I don't feel like I'm getting anywhere. I'm just caught in a rut.

<Jesus> Whenever UR caught in a rut, it's important to look up to higher ground. I'm glad U chose to connect with Me.

<TEEN> How will connecting with U help?

<Jesus> Well, when your eyes are fixed on Me, it helps U keep in mind what's really important.

<TEEN> Like what?

<GOD> Like all the things I stand for: honesty, peace, love, power, meaning, salvation, and a ton of other great things. I'm all about U carrying on your daily responsibilities, but I'm not about U getting lost in them. Just look to Me, and I'll help U do more than just get through the day—I'll help U find the awesome mystery of living.

If people can't see what God is doing,
they stumble all over themselves; but
when they attend to what he reveals,
they are most blessed.

proverbs.29:18.msg

You've got to shoot for something. Without a vision, the people fall apart; and without a goal to run towards, you will just be running around in circles. That's why you've got to get into My Word, the Bible—it gives you the road map and the target to shoot for. Olympic swimmers keep their eyes on the marker at the end of their lane to keep their path as straight as possible. Even though they are under-water and flailing their arms and legs, this marker helps them keep their "eyes on the prize."

In the same way, you can fix your eyes on Me. Even though you may be paddling like crazy in the pool of life, don't take your eyes off of Me and the finish that will bring you glory. Read about the way I lived, talked, and acted. Everything I did was for a purpose, and every action led toward My ultimate goal—the salvation of mankind. If you live your life with this goal, it may be dangerous and wild; but it will never be dull and meaningless. Keep your eyes on Me, and you will never be stuck in a rut.

Your Goal,
Jesus

Keep Your
Eyes on God

We Can
Work It Out

LOGON>>

<TEEN> God, I've got something to say, but U won't like it.

  <GOD> Try Me.

  <TEEN> I'm really, really mad at U! Things at school stink. Things at home stink. It's like the more I follow U, the worse it gets :(

  <GOD> Go on . . .

  <TEEN> Well, can I even talk to U like that? I mean, U probably hate me now.

  <GOD> Nope. Actually, I'm glad U told Me.

  <TEEN> ???

  <GOD> Now that you've finally told Me about your problems, we can work it out. I have answers for U, but I can't help U until U bring them to Me.

I say to God my Rock,
"Why have you forgotten me?
Why must I go about mourning,
oppressed by the enemy?"

psalm.42:9.niv

King David was a man after My own heart. That means he was into the things I was into. He wanted to please Me. Yet he also wrote Psalm 42. He asks Me, flat out, "Why have You forgotten Me?" Of course, I hadn't forgotten him. But David surely felt that I had. I didn't strike him down with lightning for being mad at Me. I heard his prayers and answered them.

You see, I know everything—which means I even know what you are thinking. If you are mad at Me, I already know it. So you might as well tell Me. If you pout and sulk and keep it to yourself, I can't help you.

So bring it on. Are you mad at Me? Let Me know (because I already know anyway). You won't hurt My feelings. I'm God. I do have an answer for you. Sometimes when you are mad at Me, it's for something I didn't even do. Other times, I am working in your life, but at least we can talk about it. Talk to Me. Listen to Me. We can work it out. I want you to come to Me at your best and at your worst. I want to know the whole you. I love you madly, and nothing you say or do can ever change that.

Your Counselor,
God

A True Original

LOGON>>

<TEEN> God, I am feeling down.

<GOD> What's Up?

<TEEN> There is this person in my class who is the best at everything.

<GOD> Is that really true?

<TEEN> Well, they're better looking than I am and better at sports.

<GOD> There will always be someone who is better than U at something.

<TEEN> How do I deal with it?

<GOD> Just be the best U that U can be. There is no one else like U. I made U special.

<TEEN> But what if being me still doesn't make me the best.

<GOD> It's not about being the best at something. It's about being U.

Thank you for making me so wonderfully complex!
It is amazing to think about. Your workmanship
is marvelous—and how well I know it.

p s a l m . 1 3 9 : 1 4 . t l b

Somebody once said that comparison is the thief of joy. In other words, if you're always comparing yourself to other people, then you'll never be happy. That's because I created each person as a one of a kind, and for a one-of-a-kind purpose. Of course you aren't like anyone else; you're YOU.

It's easy to look at someone else and say, "I wish I were like them," but that's a waste of time. The best way to use your energy and time is to find out who you are, and then become the best YOU that you can. Don't waste your life trying to make yourself into a cheap imitation of someone else. Just be yourself. I love you just the way you are—a true original!

Your Maker,
God

Just Be Yourself

I've Got It Covered

LOGON>>

\<TEEN\> God, I'm freaking out!

\<GOD\> Yes, I can see that. What is it?

\<TEEN\> So many things are out of my control. Tests, relationships, life in general.

\<GOD\> That's true. UR out of control.

\<TEEN\> So is that a bad thing?

\<GOD\> Not necessarily. I AM the only person truly in control of everything.

\<TEEN\> So if UR in control of everything, then why am I freaking out?

\<GOD\> Good question. Why don't U tell me, issue by issue, the things UR worried about. Leave your worries with me, and I really will help you take care of them.

\<TEEN\> Can I trust U?

\<GOD\> Absolutely. If U want to have any peace at all, then lean on Me.

Blessed is the man [whose] delight is in the law of the LORD,
and on his law he meditates day and night.
He is like a tree planted by streams of water,
which yields its fruit in season and whose leaf does not wither.
Whatever he does prospers.

psalm.1:1-3.niv

Some people trust in money; then the stock market crashes, and they lose all of it in a day. Some people trust in power, and then they are fired or voted out of office. Some people trust in fame, and then their fans leave them for the next new celebrity. Nobody knows what the future will bring, and this makes lots of people nervous. So they try to make their lives "secure." But the only security anybody has is Me.

Think about it—I made time; I control the universe; I know the future. That's why they call Me God! If you trust in Me, then you don't ever have to worry. Things might not turn out exactly the way you planned, but I am in control, and I love you. There is a song that says, "Many things about tomorrow I don't seem to under- stand; but I know who holds tomorrow, and I know who holds my hand." If you're anx- ious about something, pray! Ask Me to help. I will. So many people (even Christians) run around worrying about so many things. If you truly know Me and trust Me, you can pray and leave your worries with Me. I will take your prayers and answer them. I will give you My peace, and you can relax.

Your Peace,
God

Trust IN GOD

Walk On

LOGON>>

\<TEEN> Jesus, why do bad things happen in my life?

\<Jesus> U want to tell Me about what's going on with U right now?

  \<TEEN> Yeah, I'm really hurting, and it just seems like life is kind of picking on me.

    \<Jesus> A lot of times bad things happen, and they don't seem to make sense right away. But if U keep your head up and walk through them, the answers will come.

    \<TEEN> But it hurts so bad, and I want to know right now why these things are happening.

    \<Jesus> I felt the same way. In the Garden of Gethsemane, I asked My Father to take the Cross away; but then I said the huge words, "Not My will but Yours be done."

    \<TEEN> So You're saying that sometimes The Father wants me to suffer?

   \<Jesus> I'm saying that sometimes U R molded best by the things that press down on U. I love U. You've just got to trust Me enough to walk on through it.

Let us fix our eyes on Jesus, the author and perfecter of our faith, who for the joy set before him endured the cross, scorning its shame, and sat down at the right hand of the throne of God.

hebrews.12:2.niv

Whenever you need inspiration to keep you going in tough times, just look at the road that I walked to the Cross. I was set up for a crime I didn't commit, beaten within an inch of My life, and made fun of. Then I was forced to carry My own cross to the place where the Romans nailed Me to it and then left Me there to die.

Why did I do it, and why did My Father let it happen? Because My Father knew the end result would provide a way for all mankind to be restored to Him. Sometimes in your life bad stuff is going to happen—bad stuff that you can't explain and that you won't be able to find any easy answers to. But sometimes amazing results can come out of bad situations. As you know, I was killed, but I was raised from the dead; and now every man and woman can be raised with Me to live forever in Heaven. So when you feel as if you just can't go on, and you're asking, "Why does this stuff always have to happen to me?" just look to Me and draw the strength to walk on through the pain to a place of new life. I'll be with you. I promise.

Your Brother,
Jesus

The Ride
of Your Life

LOGON>>

    <TEEN> God, why am I here?

    <GOD> Don't U know?

    <TEEN> No. I feel like I'm good for nothing. I feel like I'm just here on the planet taking up space):

    <GOD> Nothing could be further from the truth. U R here on a mission.

    <TEEN> Mission Impossible :-(

    <GOD> Actually, that's about right. I've got a life of amazing adventures for U. And U R the only one in the whole world who can fulfill this particular mission.

    <TEEN> So what's the mission?

    <GOD> Keep following Me and listening to Me, and I'll fill U in on the details as we go. Believe me, U R in for a ride!

"For I know the plans I have for you,"
declares the LORD , "plans to prosper you
and not to harm you, plans to
give you hope and a future."
jeremiah.29:11.niv

You are no accident. I knew about you a long time before you were born. Not only are you unique, but My plans for you are unique. I have things for you to accomplish here on earth that nobody can accomplish but you. Just like a train is made to run on a track, I have built you to follow the path I made for you. Along the way, there will be all the adventure and excitement that you could ever imagine.

But you have to let Me lead. You'll never find My path on your own. If you do things your own way, you'll miss My turns on the path. You may even wind up somewhere that looks good, but you'll miss out on My wonderful plan for you and you'll never be truly happy. A lot of people think My plan is to ruin their lives. Nothing could be further from the truth. I plan to give you a life of great challenge and fulfillment. And the best part is, it's tailor-made for you. Trust Me, follow Me, and let the adventure begin.

Your Leader,
God

Follow God's LEAD

U Can Do It!

LOGON>>

<TEEN> Jesus, I'm feeling discouraged again.

<JESUS> What about?

<TEEN> Everything. I have all these things I'm supposed to do, and everybody expects me to know what I'm doing; but half the time I feel like I'm just making it up as I go along.

<JESUS> You've tried your power, but have U tried My power?

<TEEN> ???

<JESUS> I didn't die on the Cross just so U could go through life feeling like a failure. I'm here to help U succeed. The next time U have to do something tough, remember that I live inside U, and I can succeed through U.

<TEEN> No way!

<JESUS> Way.

I can do all things through Christ who strengthens me.

philippians.4:13.nkjv

When you accept Me as your Lord and Savior, I come into your heart—I move into you in the same way you move into a house. I walked on the water, calmed the storm, endured the torture of the Cross, and defeated death and the devil. And now I'm living inside you.

Do you feel scared, afraid, unqualified? Do you feel like you're the wrong one for the job? The good news is, it's not about you. It's about Me living inside you. If you let Me, I will succeed through you every time. Do you have to give a speech? I can give you confidence. Do you have to run a race? I can give you strength. And if things don't work out exactly the way you thought they would, as long as you are doing your best, that's all you can do. The good news is, I love you no matter what happens.

I'm the Miracle Man. I love you, and I'm here to catch you when you fall. No matter what happens, you will live forever in Heaven, and we'll have an awesome time. So go for it! You can do it!

Your Strength,
Jesus

Go On God's Power

U Can Close Your Eyes; It's All Right.

LOGON>>

<TEEN> God, please help me.

<GOD> What is it?

<TEEN> I just feel beaten down. I just want to curl up and hide.

<GOD> I totally understand. U don't have to explain why. U can hide in Me.

<TEEN> How?

<GOD> U can't see Me, but I am more real than anything U can see, and I am there with U now. Be still and let Me hold U. Lean your heart into Me. I'm not as far away as U think.

The LORD your God is with you, he is mighty to save.
He will take great delight in you,
he will quiet you with his love,
he will rejoice over you with singing.
z e p h a n i a h . 3 : 1 7 . n i v

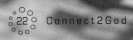

Have you ever been sick on a cold day? All you want is to be bundled up in a warm comforter and be served hot chicken soup. Most people long to be comforted when things are tough—you want someone to hold you close, to sing you to sleep, and to whisper that everything's going to be all right. Some people have earthly parents who comfort them like this. Some people don't. But I am your Heavenly Father, and My heart longs to comfort you.

People often spend so much time running around trying to please Me. They put on a brave face, but many times they are broken and hurting inside. You may have to act tough with other people, but you don't have to act tough with Me. You can let down your guard. I will never hurt you. All I want to do is hold you close and sing you songs of love. Be still and receive My love. You are My precious, precious child. I love you more than words can say.

Your Loving Father,
God

Don't Give Up

LOGON>>

<TEEN> God, sometimes I feel that I don't have the energy to keep on going.

<GOD> Everybody feels like that sometimes. Everyone feels stressed out at times.

<TEEN> Yeah, but some of my friends even talk about ending it all and killing themselves.

<GOD> That's where it falls apart. There's always an opportunity to despair, but it is never worth it to totally give up hope.

<TEEN> So what do I say to my friends who talk about ending it all?

<GOD> The best thing U can share with them is the hope that U have in your relationship with Me. And be real with them about the times that U almost gave up, but kept on going instead.

In your hearts set apart Christ as Lord. Always be prepared to give an answer to everyone who asks you to give the reason for the hope that you have. But do this with gentleness and respect.

1peter.3:15.niv

What if you wrote an awesome movie script, and a major motion picture company decided to make it into a multimillion-dollar movie? As in all movies, there is a lot of trouble and turmoil in the movie characters' lives. But then comes this amazing part where the characters learn from their problems and understand why they are alive. Sounds like a pretty good movie, huh? Well, what if while filming the troubling part of the movie, all the actors quit, saying it was too hard—that their characters' parts were too heavy a burden for them to bear? It would frustrate you because you, as the writer, would know that the good part is just around the corner.

Sometimes real life is difficult. The world is broken and acting out in the pains of its sinful condition. And sometimes people get hurt. But you've got to hold on and encourage your friends to hold on also. Everything seems huge when you're going through it, but don't give up hope. Wait for the next scene and hold on. I will be there with you because I am the author and producer of this life. And if you walk with Me, that amazing part will come.

The Author of Life,
God

Just Hold On

Feed Your Head

LOGON>>

<TEEN> Lord, it seems like my brain is living in two different worlds.

<GOD> What do U mean?

<TEEN> Sometimes I think about U and church; but then other times I think about TV and bands and movies and school.

<GOD> How are those worlds different?

<TEEN> Well, You're always telling me to love people, but it seems like everybody else is telling me to be cool, or buy certain things, or act a certain way.

<GOD> Right. So which world is best for your brain?

<TEEN> Your world, but I can't just go to another planet and focus on U. How do I do it?

Let God transform you into a new person by changing the way you think. Then you will know what God wants you to do.

romans.12:2.nlt

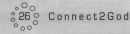

<<DOWNLOAD

Everything you do starts in your mind as a thought. When you get a snack from the refrigerator, it starts with the thought, I'm hungry. Watch a bunch of food commercials on TV, and guess what—you're going to wind up eating more. That's just the way it works. If you can control your mind, you can control your actions.

The bad news is, you live in a world full of people, corporations, entertainers, and politicians who don't care anything about Me. And they are constantly bombarding your mind with messages that go against My nature. The good news is, you can choose to listen to Me instead. Spend more time reading the Bible and turn off the TV. I want to change the way you think. I want to share My wonderful plans for you. I want to comfort you and give you hope. Ask Me, and I will begin to change your world, beginning with your mind.

Your Transformer,
God

God Is in Control

Friends Are Worth It

LOGON>>

<TEEN> Lord, my best friend is acting weird. I call her, but no answer. It's like she doesn't even want to talk to me.

<GOD> She's probably going through a hard time.

<TEEN> Well, how does that help me? :(

<GOD> It's not always about U. ;-) Hang in there with her and pray for her. When she's ready, she will come around. Good friends are worth the effort.

Two people can accomplish more
than twice as much as one. . . .
If one person falls,
the other can reach out and help.

e c c l e s i a s t e s . 4 : 9 - 1 0 . n l t

Some people think of themselves as loners. It's them against the world, and they don't need any help. But even the Lone Ranger had a partner! Two people can accomplish tasks that a single person simply can't accomplish. A team of two carpenters can finish building a house much faster than a single carpenter.

Friends are especially helpful when it comes to your feelings, your thoughts, and your emotions. A friend can help you sort things out. Nobody is perfect, so don't waste your time searching for the perfect friend. Find friends who believe in Me, who will help you when things get tough, and then stick with them. "Friends come and friends go, but a true friend sticks by you like family" (Proverbs 18:24 MSG).

 You can't control your friends, but you can control yourself. Decide to stick with your friends even in the tough times, no matter what.

Your Friend,
God

Out of the Box

LOGON>>

<TEEN> Jesus, I'm kind of embarrassed to admit this but . . .

<JESUS> Go ahead.

<TEEN> OK. I think about U when I'm at church or when I read my Bible, but then I go to school and sometimes it's like You're not even there.

<JESUS> Why would I be at church but not at school?

<TEEN> Well, at school I'll forget about U and think about homework and classmates and everything but U.

<JESUS> U probably also forget about your toes at school, but that doesn't make them disappear :-) I'm always with U, whether U remember it or not.

"For everything, absolutely everything,
above and below, visible and invisible,
. . . everything got started in [Jesus]
and finds its purpose in Him.

colossians.1:16.msg

You might think that I am just for church, that I have nothing to do with your school, or the weather, or your parents' jobs, or the rest of the world. Nothing could be further from the truth. Actually, the world exists so I can have a relationship with you. Some Christians want to keep Me in a box. They take Me out on Sunday, and then they put Me back into the box for the rest of the week.

But I won't fit into a box, and when Christians try to fit Me into a box like that, the guy in the box whom they are worshiping is not really Me! Sometimes it seems to you that the world is out of control and I'm just sitting up here watching. But I am right there with you, and I'm in control of everything. When things get crazy in your life, talk to Me. I care, I'm powerful, and I will help you—Sunday and every day.

Your Partner,
Jesus

God Is Where You Are

Growing Up Right

LOGON>>

<TEEN> God, sometimes I'm not sure why I'm here.

<GOD> Go on.

<TEEN> Well, I'm interested in all these different things, and I'm not sure who I'm supposed to grow up to be. Which of my interests are important? Who do U want me to be?

<GOD> What a wonderful question. I'm so glad U asked that! I actually know exactly who I want U to be, and I'll show U.

<TEEN> But what if I can't do it? What if I let U down?

<GOD> U won't let Me down, because I don't expect U to grow up on your own. I'm here to help U every step of the way.

The LORD will fulfill his purpose for me.
p s a l m . 1 3 8 : 8 . n i v

<<DOWNLOAD

Maybe you feel like you are nothing special, but you can't think like that. Everything I make is special, and I made you. I didn't create you to wander around and do whatever you want. I made you for a specific reason. You exist because I have things that I want you to see and do. The main thing I want you to do is get to know Me well, but it doesn't stop there.

I have made you with very specific desires and talents. You are good at certain things. You get excited about certain things. I want you to use your gifts, to enjoy your interests, to grow into the person I made you to be. Keep coming back to Me. Keep talking to Me every day. The good news is, I'm leading you. You don't have to figure out the way all by yourself. Just keep trusting Me and obeying Me, and I will do the rest.

Your Creator,
God

You Are Special

Omni-Everything

LOGON>>

<TEEN> God, do U know the future?

<GOD> Yes.

<TEEN> Do U know everything?

<GOD> Yes.

<TEEN> So U know what I'm going to do every day?

<GOD> Yes.

<TEEN> How long have U known all these things about me?

<GOD> A long, long time ;-)

You saw me before I was born
and scheduled each day of my life
before I began to breathe.
Every day was recorded in your Book!
psalm.139:16.tlb

<<DOWNLOAD

In an action movie, sometimes the scariest part isn't when you see the bad guy; it's when the bad guy is hiding in the shadows. The unknown can be a scary thing because it is beyond your sight, beyond your control. The good news for you is that I see everything—past, present, and future. I am everywhere (omnipresent). I know everything (omniscient). I am stronger than anything (omnipotent). So nothing surprises Me.

My strength and confidence can help you because you are My child and I love you, so I'm going to protect you. You may not know what the future holds, but I know. Talk to Me when you are confused; then take time to sit still and hear what I am saying. I will show you what I want you to do. If you're listening and expecting Me to help you, I can even warn you of things you need to know. If you rely on Me and trust Me, you won't always know the future, but you don't have to be afraid of it.

Your Protector,
God

God Knows Your Future

You're #1

<TEEN> God, people are always saying that humans are animals. Am I an animal?

<GOD> No, you're a person.

<TEEN> What's the difference?

<GOD> I made the animals for U. But I made U for Me. UR more important to Me than anything else in all creation.

<TEEN> Why?

<GOD> Because I made U in My image and gave U a spirit. UR My child. You're #1 with Me, and I love U.

God decided to give us life
through the word of truth
so we might be
the most important
of all the things he made.

james.1:18.ncv

<<DOWNLOAD

I made a lot of things in this universe—exploding stars, green grasshoppers, microscopic cells—but you are the most important thing I've ever made. You can know Me. You can be close to Me. You can choose to let Me change you. You can love Me back. All of nature does love Me as its creator. But you can love Me as your father and friend. This makes you different from anything else I made.

Feel important when you look around My world and see all the wonderful things I made. I did it for you. I wanted to place you in a world full of waterfalls, music, blue skies, spring flowers, fall leaves. I love looking at the world I made. It gives Me great pleasure. But even more than that, I love watching you enjoy the world I made. There is no mountaintop view, crimson sunset, or brilliant supernova that will ever compare to the amazing beauty that you are to Me. I love you madly.

Your Creator and Friend,
God

You Are the
IMAGE
OF GOD

Radical LOVE

LOGON>>

<TEEN> Jesus, I love U. Do U love me?

<JESUS> More than U will ever know.

<TEEN> How do U know that I love U? Do U believe me?

<JESUS> Yes. When U obey Me and choose to do things My way, that shows Me that U love Me. Plus, I can see your heart.

<TEEN> How can I know that U love me? I can't see Your heart.

<JESUS> If U want to see My heart of love for U, look at the Cross.

God is love.
1john.4:8.niv

These days, people use the word "love" like they use the word "cool." I love spearmint gum! I love your new haircut! My love for you is much stronger than any of that. Love is meaningless without action. I can say, "I love you," but if you're really thirsty and I don't give you a sip of My drink, then I don't really love you. I'm just talking.

Not only do I love, but I am love. Any goodness, justice, love, and mercy in the world comes from Me. I have so much love for you that I chose to suffer a horrible death for you. You had sinned, but I let the Father punish Me instead of you. I was whipped, tortured, and nailed to a cross where I surrendered to death. And I did it all for you. If you were the only person alive in the world, I still would have done it all for you. And it was 100 percent worth it. I would do it again in a second. You mean more to Me than life itself.

Your Love,
Jesus

You're Worth It

Spit It Out!

LOGON>>

<TEEN> God, I've got something to say, but I don't know how to say it.

  <GOD> You've sinned, right?

  <TEEN> How did U know?

  <GOD> I always know :) Tell Me about your sin.

  <TEEN> But I'm ashamed. Won't U be disappointed in me?

  <GOD> Actually, I'll be proud of U for telling Me. I made U, and I understand how sin works. It's not a surprise to Me. People fail. I want to help U succeed. But moping around hiding your sin from Me only makes things worse.

What happiness for those whose guilt has been forgiven! . . . What relief for those who have confessed their sins and God has cleared their record.

psalm.32:1.tlb

Sin is like poison—the longer you keep it inside, the more it eats away at your insides. Everybody sins at one point or another, and it is a big deal when you keep it to yourself. But you are only hurting yourself when you try to keep it a secret. I am ready to forgive you. I want to wipe the slate clean and give you a new start. I can't forgive you until you confess your sin and turn from it.

Understand, not every thought you have is a sin. It's only when you let that thought come in and your entertain it for a while that it becomes a sin. Not every action is a sin. If you accidentally drop a hammer on someone's head, that's not sin (but you still might want to apologize to them). If you throw a hammer at someone's head, that's a different matter. If you have sinned, tell Me right now and get it off your chest. Ask Me to forgive you. Unconfessed sin is like swallowed poison. Spit it out!

Your Forgiver,
God

You're FORGIVEN

 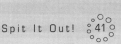

I'm Not Out to Get U

LOGON>>

<TEEN> God, can I be honest with U?

<GOD> Please do.

<TEEN> Sometimes I think You're mad at me, and it makes me afraid of U :-(

<GOD> Why would I be mad at U?

<TEEN> I can't think of any specific thing, but sometimes I just feel like UR mad.

<GOD> Even when U sin, I'm not mad at U. I hate the sin, but I love U. If I love U even when U sin, then surely I love U when you're not sinning.

<TEEN> I guess so. I just wish I could feel Your love more.

<GOD> Keep spending time with Me, and U will.

Perfect love drives out fear.

1john.4:18.niv

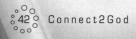

There are two kinds of fear—the good kind and the bad kind. The good kind of fear is more like respect. Hopefully, you wouldn't stick a metal fork into an electrical socket. You would have too much respect for the power of electricity. When the Bible says you should fear God, it's talking about this good kind of fear. It means that you realize I am powerful, holy, and in charge, and you show Me honor and respect.

But there is also a bad kind of fear—the constant fear of punishment. If you think I am a mean guy in Heaven waiting to throw lightning bolts at you whenever you make a mistake, then you probably won't want to spend a lot of time hanging out with Me. Please understand, I'm not like that at all. I love you more than you could ever imagine, and I'm always looking for ways to encourage you and build you up. The last thing I want to do is destroy you. Get to know Me. Read in the Bible about My relationship with Jesus. The more you know how much I love you, the less afraid of Me you'll be, and the more fun we can have.

Your Encourager,
God

GOD IS NOT
Mad at You

Get Your Hopes Up

LOGON>>

<TEEN> God, I need Your help again.

<GOD> Sure, what is it?

<TEEN> I have a big problem—so big even U might not even be able to handle it :)

<GOD> Ha! U underestimate Me. There has never been and never will be a problem too big for Me. I'm not bragging; that's just the truth.

God . . . is able to do far more than we would ever dare to ask or even dream of— infinitely beyond our highest prayers, desires, thoughts, or hopes.
ephesians.3:20.tlb

People are always saying, "Don't get your hopes up." I'm saying, "Do get your hopes up." I will never fail you. Most people trust Me until things start getting tough, and then they say, "Thanks, God, but this isn't working out like I'd hoped. I'll take over from here." But if you will just hang in there with Me, even through the tough times, you will see My miracles.

Noah trusted Me when I asked him to build a boat. That giant boat must have seemed pretty ridiculous to his neighbors, since Noah didn't live anywhere near water. And up to that point in history it had never even rained. But Noah obeyed Me and kept building the boat, and it delivered him from the Flood.

David, with nothing but a sling and some stones, took on the giant Goliath. Goliath thought David was crazy. And David's brothers thought he was crazy too. But David trusted Me anyway, and he cut off Goliath's head. Are you getting the picture? I can do much more than you think I can. Think big! Hope big! If you will obey Me and trust Me, no matter how crazy it seems, you will see My miracles.

Your Deliverer,
God

RELATIONSHIP
with God …
PRICELESS

LOGON>>

<TEEN> Father, being rich looks like fun. Is it wrong to be rich?

<GOD> Not necessarily, but being rich is not always as much fun as it seems.

<TEEN> Why?

<GOD> Because people are truly happy only when they know Me, and lots of times being rich keeps people from knowing Me.

<TEEN> How come?

<GOD> Because they trust their money to fix their problems, so they never pray and ask Me for help. Even if U have a lot of money, it's usually better to live a simple life.

A pretentious, showy life
is an empty life;
a plain and simple life is a full life.
proverbs.13:7.msg

The Beatles have a song that says, "Money can't buy me love." They were right about that. Another thing money can't buy you is happiness. Yet TV and magazines are full of flashy, showy people wearing expensive jewelry, driving fast cars, living in big houses, and they sure look like they're having fun. But when the cameras stop rolling and the crowds go home, most of those people are empty inside because they don't know Me.

Now compare those fancy people to Francis of Assisi. He owned nothing but the clothes on his back; he worked all day rebuilding churches with his bare hands; and he preached to birds and animals. He slept on the ground—not exactly *Lifestyles of the Rich and Famous.* Yet Francis was one of My happiest, most satisfied children. What was his secret? He kept his life simple and focused on Me.

There is nothing wrong with making money, but unless you put Me first, money won't solve your problems. It often creates more problems. Don't chase after money. Chase after Me. I will make your life worth living.

Your Reward,
God

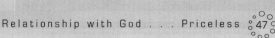

DON'T Worry–Pray

LOGON>>

<TEEN> God, I'm worried about my future.

<GOD> What about it?

<TEEN> Everything. Will I have friends? Will I be happy? What will happen to me?

<GOD> Let's talk about it.

<TEEN> Well, I've worried about it, and I'm talking about it with U right now. Is that what U mean?

<GOD> Not exactly :) It's one thing to worry about your future in My presence. But it's a much better thing to give Me your future and trust Me to take care of it. As long as you're holding on to your worries, I can't take them from U.

*You, LORD, give perfect peace
to those who keep their purpose
firm and put their trust in you.*
i s a i a h . 2 6 : 3 . t e v

You can't trust Me and worry at the same time. If you are worrying, then you aren't trusting Me. If you are truly trusting Me, then you won't worry. Imagine a man who hires armed security guards and ferocious watchdogs to guard his home day and night, but then he stays up all night worrying about burglars. That man is not taking advantage of his investment. If you're a Christian, then you have invested your trust in Me, and I've got your back. I'm watching over you. I never sleep. I guard you 24/7.

If you really trust Me, then don't worry. Every time you start worrying about something, pray about it instead. Turn your worries into prayers. After you talk to Me, ask Me to give you My peace, and wait quietly until you receive it. I will take your cares and give you My peace, but you have to let them go. No take backs. Leave them in My hands. That's the way it works. Trust Me. I am in charge.

Your Fortress,
God

Face FORWARD

LOGON>>

<TEEN> Jesus, I've blown it.

<JESUS> How?

<TEEN> U know my past. I'm not really perfect. I don't always stand up for U. How can U use me to do anything good?

<JESUS> When U ask Me to forgive U, it's a new, fresh start. When U allow Me to live through U, U can do all things.

Forgetting what is behind and straining toward what is ahead, I press on toward the goal to win the prize for which God has called me heavenward in Christ Jesus.

philippians.3:13-14.niv

Your past is over and done with. There is nothing you can do to get it back. You may have done some horrible things. You may have even done some horrible things yesterday. But if you ask Me to forgive you, and if you're willing to start over again, then I will forget your past. You have a clean slate. I have great plans for your future, and you might miss them if you sit around worrying about your past.

When I was arrested and crucified, My friend Peter turned his back on Me and swore he didn't even know Me. But when I rose from the dead, I met Peter on the shores of Galilee where we grew up, and I forgave him and changed him. Peter went on to become the main preacher of the Jerusalem church. Then he was arrested, tortured, and killed just as I was, all for saying that I was God. Peter blew it the first time; but he died unashamed, praising Me, telling everyone that I was his friend.

I am less interested in your past mistakes and more interested in your future successes. You are NOT disqualified. Forget about your past and go for it!

Your Goal,
Jesus

Begin Again
NOW

ONE WAY

LOGON>>

<TEEN> Jesus, I heard somebody say that all roads lead to God . . . Buddha, Mohammed. Some people say all these guys are just as good as U.

<JESUS> People say all sorts of things. But the Bible—God's very own Word—says I'm the only way to God.

<TEEN> How can U say You're the only way, when all these other religions say there are many ways?

<JESUS> I can confidently say that I'm the only way, because I know who I am. I'm not a man guessing at how to reach God. I AM God.

"I am the way and the truth and the life.
No one comes to the Father except through me."
j o h n . 1 4 : 6 . n i v

Before I came to earth, whenever God the Father wanted to really get somebody's attention, He would send an angel, or speak in a dream, or show up in a burning bush. But nobody could really see Him face-to-face because God the Father is Spirit. He doesn't have a physical body. I came to earth so that people could see God the Father better. If you want to know God the Father, then get to know Me.

Read about My life in the Bible. See what I am like. I am God with skin on. My Father wanted to make a way for you to really know Him. He built a bridge between humans and himself. I am that bridge. All other religious leaders were just men. I'm a man too, but not just a man. I am the Father's only Son, and I myself am God. You can read about Buddha and his accomplishments while he lived on the earth, but he can't lead you to the Father's heart. There is one bridge between humans and their Creator, and I am that bridge.

Your Way,
Jesus

KNOW JESUS; Know God

What LASTS?

LOGON>>

<TEEN> Jesus, who is the richest man in the world?

<JESUS> It depends on how U define "rich."

<TEEN> OK. How do U define it?

<JESUS> A truly rich person has a heart that can't wait to obey the Father. That person's treasure is in loving other people.

<TEEN> So money doesn't have anything to do with being rich?

<JESUS> Not unless U use your money to love people.

We fix our eyes not on what is seen,
but on what is unseen.
For what is seen is temporary,
but what is unseen is eternal.
2corinthians.4:18.niv

Perhaps you've heard people say about material things, "You can't take it with you." No matter how much money or stuff you get, when you die, you have to leave it all on earth. The richest millionaire goes into eternity as naked as the poorest beggar.

Although you can't take physical things with you to Heaven, you can take spiritual things. Every time you help a friend or feed someone who is hungry or obey your parents—you can take all those things to Heaven. Such acts of love and obedience change your spirit. They make you more like Me. And your spirit is the part of you that lives forever in Heaven. When you think about things from that perspective, spending money to help other people is actually the best long-term investment you can make.

Focus on these spiritual "treasures"— loving people, serving people, telling them about My love, just listening to people and being kind to them—and you will be "rich" in Heaven.

Your Reward,
Jesus

Think
Long-Term

 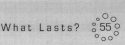

God Is in the Details

<TEEN> I need something interesting to do.

<GOD> Like what?

<TEEN> Something extra like chess, music, or acting. I'm ready to explore more of what life has to offer.

<GOD> Excellent! Make Me a part of it. Let's explore together.

Make a careful exploration of who you are and the work you have been given, and then sink yourself into that.

galatians.6:4.msg

<<DOWNLOAD

I have buried amazing mysteries deep within life, and I want you to discover them. A great architect named Mies once said, "God is in the details." As you get into the details of life, you will find Me there. Get into biology, and you will discover Me in the plan of nature. Get into math, and you will discover Me in the precision of systems. Get into music, and you will discover Me in the passion and majesty of rhythm and melody that words cannot contain. I have designed you to discover particular details about My world.

First, think about what kind of things you enjoy—pottery, politics, accounting, engineering, bee-keeping, carpentry, ballet. . . . Next, think about what you do well. Finally, pray and see what I think. Then, pick something and get into it. Learn about it. Take classes after school, read books, talk to older people who are experts. I made an exciting world full of things for you to master. So pick something and start getting deep into it.

Your Master Architect,
God

Your
Hiding Place

LOGON>>

<TEEN> Father, kids were picking on me today, making fun of me. I didn't cry, but I felt like crying.

<GOD> I was there. I saw what happened, and it breaks My heart. U can cry to Me about it if U like. It's all right.

<TEEN> I feel that if I start crying at all, I will totally fall apart.

<GOD> It's OK. U can fall apart with Me. Nobody will see. When you're with Me, U can be vulnerable. I won't make fun of U. I will protect U. U don't have to be strong with Me.

My soul finds rest in God alone;
my salvation comes from him.
He alone is my rock and my salvation;
he is my fortress, I will never
be shaken.
p s a l m . 6 2 : 1 - 2 . n i v

<<DOWNLOAD

I am a hiding place for you when times get tough. I'm offering a refuge, a protected place of retreat and peace, a place where your enemies can't get you.

You don't have to handle everything all by yourself. When it feels like the world is a strong hurricane swirling around you, you don't have to stand your ground alone. Run to Me. Pour your heart out to Me, and let Me comfort you. I'm listening. I am powerful enough to protect you and to love you. But you have to come to Me. Here you can let down your guard. You may have to put on a brave face with other people, but not with Me. With Me, you can simply be My child. I will hold you and comfort you. I will protect you. I am strong enough and I am willing.

Your Fortress,
God

Stuff Is
Just Stuff

LOGON>>

<TEEN> Is it wrong to want stuff? Cars, money, clothes . . .

<GOD> It depends on what that stuff means to U. When your stuff becomes so important that it takes the place of Me, then it's wrong.

<TEEN> But how can that happen?

<GOD> When your stuff is your main source of peace, protection, comfort, and satisfaction, then UR worshiping your stuff, and UR not worshipping Me.

"No servant can serve two masters. . . . You cannot serve both God and Money."

luke.16:13.niv

<<DOWNLOAD

Greedy people simply can't seem to get enough. In your generation, this problem is called "materialism." It means relying on "stuff" to meet your spiritual needs. The thinking goes like this: "If I can get just one more car, one more piece of jewelry, a bigger home—then I will finally be satisfied." But material things alone can't satisfy.

If you trust in your stuff to make you happy, you will always be disappointed. Whichever god you trust most, that's the god you serve. You're either trusting Me, or you're trusting your stuff. I am the only one who can truly satisfy. Satisfaction is a gift from Me. If you are trusting in Me, and you do get some new stuff, you can enjoy it because you're thinking about it in the right way.

Your Satisfaction,
Jesus

Jesus Is True
Satisfaction

BE REAL

LOGON>>

<TEEN> Father, I'm ashamed of myself :-(

<GOD> What about?

<TEEN> Well, I'm not as smart as a lot of other people. I struggle with things other people can do so easily.

<GOD> I'm so glad U came to Me. Just be honest about who U are, and I will make up the difference.

He said to me,

"My grace is sufficient for you,

for My strength is made perfect in weakness."

Therefore most gladly

I will rather boast in my infirmities,

that the power of Christ may rest upon me.

2corinthians.12:9.nkjv

I want you to be as strong as you can be, but I don't want you to fake it. Don't pretend that you can do more than you can. Don't be ashamed of where you are. Don't be ashamed of your limitations. I actually use your limitations to display My power.

Pretend you are a weight lifter, and the most you can lift is 200 pounds. You enter a competition, and miraculously I help you lift 400 pounds. If everybody knows your limits, they will ask, "How on earth did you do it?"

And you can say, "It was God. It was a miracle!" Then everyone will know My power. But if you lie and say, "Oh, yeah, it was me. I've lifted that lots of times," then you steal the credit and nobody sees My power. I don't want you to be weak on purpose. I just want you to be honest about your limitations. Don't be ashamed of them. I show up best when you keep it real.

Your Power,
God

Don't Fight, RUN.

LOGON>>

<TEEN> Jesus, why do I sometimes want to do things I'm not supposed to do?

<JESUS> It's just part of life. I was tempted too, just like U.

<TEEN> How did U keep from sinning?

<JESUS> Temptation is like a giant wad of bubble gum—the more U fight it, the more caught up U get, until you're stuck in sin.

<TEEN> So how do U beat it?

<JESUS> U can't beat temptation by wrestling it. U have to run away from it.

"God keeps his promise, and he will not allow you to be tested beyond your power to remain firm; at the time you are put to the test, he will give you the strength to endure it, and so provide you with a way out."

1corinthians.10:13.tev

Temptation is part of life. I was tempted just like you are. But I never sinned, and you don't have to either. Temptation is not sin. It's just a suggestion for you to disobey God. When temptation presents itself, look for a way out of it. If you have to, run away. Leave the tempting situation. You cannot overcome a temptation by staring it down. The more you think about a temptation, the more you want to do it. The dieter who is tempted to snack doesn't go to a candy store and stare at the chocolate bars until she has overcome temptation. She stays as far away from the candy store as possible.

When I was in the desert, the devil tempted Me three times. Each time, I didn't argue with him. I told him what God had to say about it in the Bible. Finally, the devil left Me. The more you resist temptation, the easier it is to resist it the next time. When you are tempted, connect with Me. I know what you are going through. Ask Me to help you. Then look for My way out, and take it quickly.

Your Strength & Wisdom,
Jesus

Turn Your Back to Sin

When Parents DON'T Understand

LOGON>>

<TEEN> Hey, God—U there?

<GOD> I AM. What's on your mind?

<TEEN> Why don't my parents understand I need to be me?

<GOD> Do U understand them?

<TEEN> No way!

<GOD> There will always be someone in your life who doesn't understand you.

<TEEN> What do I do?

<GOD> Pray for them. Listen to them. Ask Me for wisdom. I can give U insight. And . . . .

<TEEN> And?

<GOD> And I understand U, and I love U for who U R.

<TEEN> Yeah?

<GOD> Since I created U, I know U inside and out.

<TEEN> Thx, God. It's good to know that somebody understands me.

Thank you for making me so wonderfully complex! It is amazing to think about. Your workmanship is marvelous —and how well I know it.

psalm.139:14.tlb

You can come to Me with any problems—even when it's your parents. They often have a different perspective than you do. The first thing you can do is pray for them. Parenting isn't a skill they were born with, and it is really as hard for them as it is for you. Next, be a good listener. Forgive them when you think they're wrong, the way I always forgive you when you make mistakes. When you give parents your attention, love, and understanding, it grows; and you will find that they can become more attentive to you, loving and understanding.

But even when parents understand you, remember that there will always be people in your life who don't understand you. You can make it through life happily if you remember that I know who you are and I love who you are. After all, I designed you, and many of your unique features are gifts I gave to you for us to enjoy. You are valuable and precious to Me and to others.

So when others don't understand, remember that communication is key. Listen . . . listen . . . listen . . . and pray. Tell Me the things that you want to see changed in them—and in you! And never forget that I understand.

Your Heavenly Father,
God

God Gets YOU

Totally Forgotten

LOGON>>

\<TEEN> God, I feel so bad about what I did the other day.

\<GOD> What do U mean? I don't know what U R talking about.

\<TEEN> Don't U remember me confessing it to U? I remember; it makes me feel bad.

\<GOD> I don't. Once U confess to Me what U did and I forgive U, I forget it.

\<TEEN> U don't remember any of it?

\<GOD> No. It's gone. In My book, it's as if U never did it.

\<TEEN> Totally forgotten?

\<GOD> Yes. I love U. Why would I want to remember what hurts U?

\<TEEN> I wish I could forgive myself like that.

\<GOD> U can.

\<TEEN> How?

\<GOD> When U give it up, U have to let it go and remember that Jesus already paid for your sins.

\<TEEN> And I don't ever have to think about it again?

\<GOD> Right.

\<TEEN> God, U R AWESOME! Thx.

"I, even I, am he who blots out your transgressions, for my own sake, and remembers your sins no more."

isaiah.43:25.niv

<<DOWNLOAD

Sometimes it's good to forget. Most people spend a lifetime trying to remember things, but when it comes to forgiveness, I always forget whatever it is that you've done as soon as you tell Me about it and ask Me for forgiveness.

When you tell Me about all the things you feel bad about and make a decision to turn away from them, I forgive you. Even if you think it's a small thing—like a thought that you shouldn't think—when you tell me, I forgive you. I erase it as if it had never existed.

When you bring it up again, I haven't a clue what you're talking about. It doesn't exist anymore. I guess you could say it's a good form of forgetfulness. So, tell Me all about it, and ask for forgiveness. I'll forgive you, and then neither of us has to remember it again.

Your Forgiver,
God

Celebrate
with Me

LOGON>>

<TEEN> Father, do U like parties?

<GOD> Sure. Every time somebody becomes a Christian on earth, we have a massive party in Heaven.

<TEEN> I just can't see U hanging out at a party.

<GOD> Think about this. The first miracle Jesus ever did was to help keep a party going at a wedding. As U get to know Me a little better, you'll realize I know how to have a good time.

God . . . generously gives us everything for our enjoyment.
1timothy.6:17.tev

Lots of people think that if they give up their lives and follow Me, I will make them eat dirt and live in a bug-infested hut. That just doesn't make any sense. I created joy, beauty, dancing, excitement, thrills, and pleasure. The devil didn't make up these things. I did. The devil only knows how to distort and mess up the things I made.

When I created Adam and Eve, I wanted them to enjoy the Garden of Eden. When I created you, I wanted you to enjoy your life on earth. We both know life on earth is not one continuous party, but I can help you have a good time. I want to be included in everything you do. I want to be part of your whole life. And if you feel awkward including Me in some of your "fun" activities, then maybe they're not what I would agree is fun. I made you, and I know what will bring you the most joy. Include Me in your work and in your play.

Your Joy,
God

DANCE Out LOUD!

Get the Picture?

LOGON>>

<TEEN> I've got to write this poem for class, and I'm all out of ideas.

<GOD> All U have to do is ask Me to give U some.

<TEEN> U can't do that, can U? That would be like cheating. Plus, wouldn't that just be a waste of Your time?

<GOD> R U kidding? I love poetry. I was into art and creativity before the world even began. I created creativity! Every truly creative idea that anybody ever had started with Me.

The heavens declare the glory of God;
the skies proclaim the work of his hands.

psalm.19:1.niv

If you ever need a reminder of My creativity and power, just look up. When was the last time you sat and watched the clouds roll by or looked at the stars? Take some time to look around you at nature and think about the world I made. The same way you can look at a painting and appreciate something about the artist, you can look at nature and appreciate something about Me. Nature is My artistic expression.

Notice, no two stars are the same, no two clouds are the same, no two leaves are the same, and no two sunsets are the same. I have been making sunsets on earth since I started the planet spinning, and every day I make a new one. Get the picture? I never run out of ideas. I am infinitely creative and infinitely beautiful. Do you need a miracle in your life? Do you need a new idea or a new plan? Come to Me, pray, and ask Me to help. I am in the business of making all things new.

Your Creative Creator,
God

Let God Inspire You

EVERYBODY
Needs My Help

LOGON>>

<TEEN> Jesus, am I the only one who ever sins?

<JESUS> What makes U think that?

<TEEN> Well, there are some kids at church who seem so perfect.

<JESUS> I am the only one who is perfect. But U can be made perfect through Me. That's why I had to die on the Cross. I take away your sins, and I give U My perfection. I am the one true hope for every person on the planet.

All have sinned and
fall short of the glory of God.
romans.3:23.niv

<<DOWNLOAD

No one can honestly say they never sinned and don't need My forgiveness. I was the only perfect man. Everyone else from Adam to you has sinned. Sin means "missing the mark." It's like you're aiming at the right target, but you can't hit it. You want to love, but you don't love completely. You want to be kind, but sometimes you discover it's more difficult than you imagined.

When you sin, when you are selfish and mean to people, you fall short of My glory—short of My best for you. When you sin, confess it to Me, and I will forgive you. But don't fool yourself, and don't be fooled—everyone needs My help. Nobody is perfect. Everybody sins. It's better to go ahead and admit that, ask for help, and get it. Then I can help you live the life and hit the mark. It's a miracle, but I'm the Miracle Man.

Your Forgiveness,
Jesus

Nobody's Perfect

Love
Starts with U

LOGON>>

<TEEN> Father, there are some kids at church who drive me crazy.

<GOD> I created everyone differently, and not everybody is going to be your type.

<TEEN> Sure, but aren't Christians supposed to behave better?

<GOD> Eventually. I change the lives of those who let me, but the change begins on the inside. Sometimes it just takes awhile. They may be making big changes—U just can't see it yet.

<TEEN> So what do I do?

<GOD> U can't change them, so let Me change U. Pray for those kids, and ask Me to give U My heart of love for them. I love all My children, and I want U to love them too.

*Our love for each other proves
that we have gone from death to life.*

1john.3:14.cev

Suppose you see a sign advertising "cute, lovable puppies for sale." You go to the sale only to discover a cage full of huge, ferocious Dobermans biting and attacking each other. "Don't worry," the owner assures you, "they're actually gentle dogs." Would you believe him? Neither would I.

Yet that's what a lot of churches do. They proclaim to the world that they are full of love and tenderness, but behind the scenes they are gossiping, hurting each other's feelings, and living lives that don't reflect My true character. Who wants to go to a church like that? You might not get along with every single Christian in the world, but differences of opinion and personality are no excuse to be rude. Christians are your brothers and sisters. Regardless of how unlovable some of them are, I want you to love each other. The world is watching—expecting to see Me in you—and so am I.

Your Father,
God

Love Each Other

LOGON>>

<TEEN> Lord, what would U like from me? U have done a lot for me, and I want to give U something back.

<GOD> It makes Me proud of U to see U thinking that way.

<TEEN> Is there anything I can give U?

<GOD> U can give Me your whole life. That is what I want from U.

So then, my friends,
because of God's great mercy to us . . .
offer yourselves as a living sacrifice to God,
dedicated to his service and pleasing to him.
This is the true worship that you should offer.
romans.12:1.tev

I love it when you sing worship songs to Me. I love it when you pray and tell Me that you love Me. I love it when you give tithes and offerings to Me. All these things show that you love Me. But the greatest gift you can give Me is the gift of you.

It is a radical thing to give your whole self to Me. It means that you give Me permission to do with your life whatever I want. It's not as scary as it seems. I made you; I know you better than you know yourself; and I know how to give you the best life for you. You have to trust Me daily and let Me show you the things I want you to do next. If you are willing to give Me your whole life, pray right now and ask Me to use you however I want. Then, get ready for an adventure!

Your Pilot,
God

The
Transformer

LOGON>>

<TEEN> Holy Spirit, is it true that U R a person?

<HOLY SPIRIT> Yes. God is three people—Father, Son, and Holy Spirit, and I'm one of the three.

<TEEN> But y'all are all the same God, right?

<HOLY SPIRIT> Right. Don't try too hard to understand it. It will blow your mind. :)

<TEEN> So what is Your job? What is Your relationship to me?

<HOLY SPIRIT> My job is to help U become more like Jesus.

*As the Spirit of the Lord works within us,
we become more and more like him
and reflect his glory even more.*

2corinthians.3:18.nlt

When you become a Christian, I come to live inside you. I am the Holy Spirit, and I am always working. I'm like a 24-hour automatic car wash, except My job is to clean you from the inside out. If you cussed before you were a Christian, once I live inside you, it will be harder and harder for you to cuss. I change all sorts of things about you.

If it seems that you aren't getting any better, be patient and hang in there. I'm always working in you to change you, so don't resist Me; yield to Me, and let Me do My work. For instance, if you're watching a movie and it starts to bother you for whatever reason (violence, sex, cussing), stop watching it. That is Me on the inside of you letting you know you should turn away from those things. I want you to become like Jesus, and the good news is, you don't have to do it all by yourself. Ask Me to change you, and I will—from the inside out.

Your Transformer,
The Holy Spirit

God Is in Your Heart

Point to Me

LOGON>>

<TEEN> Father, why are some people famous and other people not?

<GOD> Sometimes fame is just an accident. And fame is not always a good thing. Someone could be famous for losing the world series or shooting the president.

<TEEN> Should I try to be famous? Do U want me to be famous?

<GOD> If I do want U to be famous for a day, a year, or however long, I will make U famous. If U find yourself in the spotlight, remember to tell people about the One who put U there :) Whatever happens, glory and fame should not be your focus—look to Me to get you where you're going in this life.

"Father, glorify your name!"

john.12:28.niv

Throughout history, humans have always wanted the glory. Even today in Hollywood, actors argue about whose name goes at the top of a movie poster. Rock bands argue about which member gets the songwriting credits. People who spend all their energy chasing glory and fame are rarely satisfied, because human glory is temporary. It never lasts. One day you are famous, and the next day someone else has taken your place.

I want you to think differently. Don't spend your energy trying to make yourself famous. Instead, turn your focus on Me. I want to help you succeed, to love others, and to live a great life. So when people are impressed with you and compliment you, tell them about Me. You can still say "thank you." But your life should always point people toward Me. Think of yourself as a sign. Nobody goes to see a sign that says "Statue of Liberty." They go to see the statue that the sign points to. You are the sign; I am the statue. If you will glorify My name, then I will make your life miraculous.

Your Focus,
God

Give God the Glory

To Know Me
Is to Love Me

LOGON>>

<TEEN> God, R U a head guy or a heart guy?

<GOD> What do U mean?

<TEEN> Well, some Christians are so smart, they can argue about U and know all the verses to back their arguments. Then some Christians sing, shout, and raise their hands in church during worship. It seems like there are two different groups. So which one R U?

<GOD> I'm God. I AM Me. I'm not in only one group. I'm a little bit of both groups. I want U to know your Bible, and I also want U to get emotional about Me.

Yet a time is coming and has now come
when the true worshippers
will worship the Father in spirit and truth,
for they are the kind of worshippers
the Father seeks.

john.4:23.niv

What does it mean to worship Me in spirit and truth? It seems that the churches these days want to do one or the other. Some churches are into emotions, feelings, and passion. Other churches are into reason, logic, and using their heads. Both groups are right! But you can't have one without the other.

If it's all about feelings but you never read My Word or understand the truth of My universe, you can get confused and forget whom you are worshipping. But if it's all about how much you know and there's never any emotion or passion, then you don't really know Me either, because I am a passionate, personal, intimate God. Read My Word and understand who I am. Then come away with Me by yourself where no one can hear you, and dance and sing loud love songs to Me. I am looking for people who will worship Me, who will obey Me, who will get to know Me, and who will share their hearts with Me. I invite you to become one of these true worshippers.

Your Father,
God

Learn and LOVE

Thank Me ANYWAY

LOGON>>

<TEEN> I had an awful day today.

<GOD> Thank Me.

<TEEN> What? U want me to thank U for my bad day?

<GOD> No, not at all. I'm sorry U had a bad day. But now is the perfect time for U to thank Me for all the good things I've done for U.

<TEEN> Honestly, God, I don't feel much like thanking U right now :-(

<GOD> I understand, but once U start thanking Me, you'll feel much better.

I will thank the LORD at all times.
My mouth will always praise him.

p s a l m . 3 4 : 1 . g w t

Here is a secret weapon for you when things get tough—thank Me! If you will begin to thank Me no matter what is happening to you, then you will soon be in a good mood. Thanking Me is not always as easy as it sounds, especially when things are difficult. But that is exactly when you need to thank Me the most!

When things are tough—you get a bad grade, your friend hurts your feelings, your parents don't understand you—thank Me. Sit down and make a list of all the good things I've done for you. Start with your life itself. Every breath you take is a gift from Me. That you were even born at all is a miracle. Then you can begin to thank Me for My world—for colors, animals, music, humor. Finally, think back on your life and thank Me for the things I've done for you personally—adopted you into My family, showed you how much I love you, put you on the road to an exciting adventure. Once you count your blessings, it will put your current situation into perspective. Then hang in there. My mercies are new every morning.

Your Provider,
God

Praise Is Power

An Audience OF ONE

LOGON>>

<TEEN> Sometimes I think I'm the only one at school who ever does homework honestly. Sometimes people cheat, and the teacher doesn't even notice.

<GOD> Does it matter if other people cheat?

<TEEN> Well, I could cheat and get away with it too. Who would know?

<GOD> I would know. UR not responsible for what other people do. But UR responsible for what U do. Even if U think your honesty doesn't matter to anyone else, it still matters to Me.

Whatever you do,
work at it with all your heart,
as working for the Lord, not for men.
colossians.3:23.niv

You may think you are doing homework for your teacher, but you are really doing homework for Me. You may think you are obeying your parents, but you are really obeying Me. All the work you do should be done as if you were going to turn it in to Me, because I am the One you are ultimately accountable to for all you do.

It's easy to cut corners and do a bad job when no one is looking. The thing is, I'm always looking. Even if no other person will ever know, I'll know. When people know you are a Christian, they watch to see how you do things. People want to know if Christians are any different. They want to see if Christians really do work for God, or if they cheat and slack off like everybody else. If you think of Me as your boss, you will always do a good job, and you will bless your employers. Then when people are looking, they will find you doing it right.

Your Boss,
God
.

I ONLY WANT
to Be with U

LOGON>>

<TEEN> Father, I've been missing U. I'm excited to talk to U again.

<GOD> Awesome! U don't know how much I love to hear that.

<TEEN> Really? It seems like U would be so busy with everybody else that U wouldn't really miss me.

<GOD> R U kidding? To me, it's like UR the only person in the universe. I count the hours until we can meet again.

<TEEN> U really love me that much?

<GOD> U bet. UR My #1 child. U mean everything to Me.

The LORD takes pleasure in his people.
psalm.149:4.tev

You may enjoy sports, music, or just relaxing on a beautiful day. I enjoy those things too, but I enjoy My children even more. Of all the things I've made—galaxies, sunsets, otters, jellyfish, horses, flowers—my favorite creations are My kids. And guess what? You are one of My kids!

I enjoy being with you. I like it when you talk to Me and ask Me questions. I like it when you listen for Me and try to hear My voice. I like watching you enjoy the world I made. Whenever you take pleasure in a song, a forest, or a photograph, I love watching you enjoy those things. I made this world for you, and I want to be part of your world. Nothing pleases Me more than to hear one of My children pray, "Lord, here I am. Meet with me." My heart races. That is what I long to hear. Spend some time with Me today. You'll be glad you did, and so will I.

Your Best Friend,
God

God Longs for YOU

JUST DO IT!

LOGON>>

<TEEN> Jesus, there has to be more to Christianity than just reading the Bible.

<JESUS> U bet there is.

<TEEN> So what else is there?

<JESUS> *Doing* the Bible! Pray for the sick to be healed. Feed the poor. Be kind to the losers. Love the unlovable people.

<TEEN> But honestly, all that seems really radical.

<JESUS> It is radical to the ultimate extreme! U will never experience anything more radical than actually doing the Bible.

Just as the body is dead without a spirit,
so also faith is dead without good deeds.

james.2:26.nlt

In chemistry class, there is a lecture phase and a lab phase. In the lecture phase, you sit and listen to a lecture about how all the chemicals are supposed to react. In lab, you roll up your sleeves and start mixing the actual chemicals to see how they do react. See the difference? The lecture is theoretical—it's how things should be. The lab is practical—it's how things actually are.

In your life, you need to study the Bible to learn My ways. That's the theoretical part, and it's not hard. Love Me with all your heart, and love everybody else as much as you can—that pleases Me. Then, I want you to actually do it. You cannot imagine the number of Christians in the world today who never put action to their faith by doing what they've learned. They never get out and feed anyone, they never pray for anybody, they never tell anybody about Me or My love. Don't just know what I want. Do it! Then you will see My real power in your life and in your world.

Your Lab Instructor,
Jesus

Walk It OUT

Unconditional LOVE

LOGON>>

<TEEN> God, I had a good day today. I really think I obeyed U and loved people.

   <GOD> Awesome. I'm proud of U.

   <TEEN> Do U love me more today than U did yesterday?

   <GOD> Nope.

   <TEEN> Even if I had a bad day yesterday?

   <GOD> Even if U disobeyed Me all day long yesterday.

   <TEEN> How come?

   <GOD> Because My love doesn't depend on U. It depends on Me. No matter what U do, I will never stop loving U.

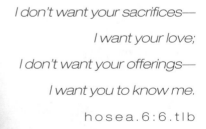

I don't want your sacrifices—
I want your love;
I don't want your offerings—
I want you to know me.
h o s e a . 6 : 6 . t l b

My dear child, you need to understand this one very important thing—I love you no matter what. Yes, I am proud of the good things that you do, but they do not make Me love you. You could do eight million good things every day until you die, and I couldn't love you any more than I already do. Even when you disobey me and I'm disappointed in your decision, I don't love you any less.

Do you get it? Do you see? It's you that I love—not what you do, but who you are. You can't earn My love. You already have it. So many Christians work too hard doing all these crazy religious things, trying to earn something that they already have. It's a waste of life! How can you be free, how can you enjoy our relationship, if you are always trying to earn a love that you already have? Relax and receive My love. It's not about what you do. It's all about Me and My love for you. Yes, keep doing good things, but understand that I love you when you succeed and when you fail. I just love you.

Your Proud Father,
God

GET INTO ME

LOGON>>

<TEEN> Father, I love U, but sometimes I wonder how much.

<GOD> I know how much, and U still have a ways to go :)

<TEEN> It's like people stand up and cheer at a football game, but U don't see people stand up and cheer for U in church.

<GOD> Well, it depends on what church you're talking about ;-), but yes, you're right. I'd like to see U get into Me a whole lot more.

"'Love the Lord your God with all your heart and with all your soul and with all your mind.' This is the first and greatest commandment."

matthew.22:37-38.niv

Do you know the term "halfhearted?" It means that you're not really giving it your all; you'd rather be somewhere else. If you're halfhearted about baseball, it's not your main thing. It's just something that's OK.

Now think about the term "wholehearted." If you're wholehearted about ballet, then you are into it 100 percent. Before rehearsal starts, you are there stretching and warming up. After rehearsal is over, you stay behind to practice on your own. When you get home, you watch ballet videos and listen to ballet music. You eat, sleep, and breathe ballet! I want you to be wholehearted about Me. What will that look like? Let Me show you. It's not something that you can fake. It has to come from your heart. I am actually more exciting than ballet, or baseball, or any hobby you could ever imagine. If you don't feel wholehearted about Me, connect with Me and expect Me to change your heart. I want you to be way into Me. I am way into you.

Your One Thing,
God

I Am
Always with U

LOGON>>

<TEEN> Jesus, when bad things happen to me, where R U?
Don't U care?

<JESUS> I am right there with U, holding U. I care more
than U can imagine.

<TEEN> Then why do U allow evil to happen? Why don't U
just stop it?

<JESUS> Actually, I stop a great deal of evil that U never
see or know about. The evil that I don't stop I endured on the
Cross. People do some evil things, but I am still in control; and
I am able to repair even the worst damage.

If anyone causes one of these
little ones who believe in me to sin,
it would be better for him to be
thrown into the sea with a large
millstone tied around his neck.
mark.9:42.niv

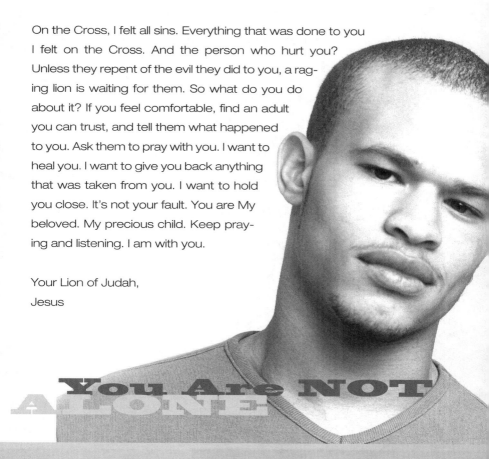

If any adult has abused you in any way, if they've hurt your body or taken advantage of you sexually, if they've yelled at you or cursed you, I want you to know that I see all things. I was there when you were harmed, and I felt what it did to you. And it makes Me furious. One of my titles is "The Lion of Judah"—a powerful king who defends his people; and I am like a raging lion when I think about any harm that was done to you.

On the Cross, I felt all sins. Everything that was done to you I felt on the Cross. And the person who hurt you? Unless they repent of the evil they did to you, a raging lion is waiting for them. So what do you do about it? If you feel comfortable, find an adult you can trust, and tell them what happened to you. Ask them to pray with you. I want to heal you. I want to give you back anything that was taken from you. I want to hold you close. It's not your fault. You are My beloved. My precious child. Keep praying and listening. I am with you.

Your Lion of Judah,
Jesus

You Are NOT ALONE

Love Is a Verb

LOGON>>

<TEEN> Jesus, I have a problem.

<JESUS> Go ahead.

<TEEN> Sometimes I want to do things Your way, but I have to be honest and admit—sometimes I don't :-(

<JESUS> UR not alone. Whenever U want to obey Me, use those times to ask Me to make U 100 percent obedient. Then when U feel like disobeying, ask Me to change your heart.

<TEEN> I thought it was all up to me. You're saying U will help me obey U?

<JESUS> Without My help, obedience is impossible.

"If you love me, you will obey my commandments."
john.14:15.tev

What if a man claims to love his wife, but he never does the dishes for her, never takes her out to a nice restaurant, never mows the lawn, and never even takes out the garbage? His actions don't demonstrate his love for her. Love is a verb. If you love, then you will do something that looks like love. Anybody can say the word love. Listen to the radio, and you'll hear love sung 20 times every hour. It's one thing to say, "I love you." It's another thing to roll up your sleeves and wash the dishes.

If you love Me, you will do what I say. You will obey Me. You won't say, "Yes, Lord, but I think I'm going to do it my way instead." You were born wanting to disobey Me. Adam and Eve disobeyed Me in the Garden, and humans have found difficulty in obedience ever since. You need My help to change your heart, to make you obedient. If you feel disobedient, but you want to obey Me, then pray. I love you, and I want to help you love Me—not just in what you say, but in what you do.

Your Helper,
Jesus

Put Your Love into Action

The RIGHT STEPS

LOGON >>

<TEEN>   God, how much do U know about me?

<GOD>   **Everything.**

<TEEN>   But like today, do U know where I'm going to go
and exactly what I'm going to say and think?

<GOD>   Yes. Not only that, but I've got places that I want
U to go and things that I want U to say and think.

<TEEN>   UR really that involved?

<GOD>   Yes! I really want to be intimately included in your
daily life.

*The steps of the godly are
directed by the LORD. He delights
in every detail of their lives.*

p s a l m . 3 7 : 2 3 . n l t

I am an "up close and personal" God. I know every single thing about you. I'm not watching you from a distance; I'm not even watching you from across the room. I am in your midst. I walk with you. I sit beside you. I actually live in your heart. I even see your dreams.

If you will commit your life to Me, I can get even more involved. I see the future, and I can make things happen. If you'll let Me, I'll direct your steps today. I'll lead you where I want you to go, but you have to be willing to let Me get involved. Listen throughout the day, and you will hear Me leading you. I can tell you who to talk to; I can even tell you what to say. Does it matter which color socks you wear? Probably not (unless one is white and one is blue). But I do want to be that involved in your life. You matter a great deal to Me.

Your Partner,
God

Let God
LEAD YOU

Invest in People

LOGON>>

<TEEN> God, do U care how I spend my money?

<GOD> Definitely. It's actually My money; I'm just loaning it to U for a while.

<TEEN> Ha! OK. So what do U want me to spend Your money on?

<GOD> People. Spend it caring for people and getting to know them. U can spend your money on other stuff too, but people are the most important.

Where your treasure is,
there your heart will be also.
matthew.6:21.niv

It's easy to tell what a person cares about. Don't listen to what he says he cares about. Look at what he spends his money on. Does he spend his money on cars, boats, homes, and clothes; but not a dime goes to My Church—My people? Then he doesn't care about My people. It's that simple.

People spend their money on the things that mean the most to them. I don't mind you spending money on good things. I don't even mind you having lots of money. But if you have lots of money, you should spend some of it on Me—telling people about Me, feeding people who are hungry, encouraging people to get to know Me better. Introduce people to Me, and you will see some of them in Heaven. Boats and cars wind up in the junkyard, but relationships can last forever, so invest in people.

Your Treasure,
God

Daily Decision

LOGON>>

<TEEN> Jesus, I've decided to follow U. I really have, but . . .

<JESUS> But what?

<TEEN> Well, I'm always taking it back. I do things that I don't want to do. I wind up following my own plans instead of doing it Your way. What's wrong?

<JESUS> Think about it like this—every time you come back from your regular checkup at the dentist, you "decide" you are going to floss your teeth every day. But that decision is just the beginning. You still have to wake up every day and actually floss your teeth!

"If people want to follow me, they must give up the things they want. They must be willing to give up their lives daily to follow me."
luke.9:23.ncv

It's not enough to say once and for all, "Jesus, have Your way in my life." You've got to choose the higher life every day in the small decisions you make. It's like a diet. You can decide one day, "I'm going to lose twenty pounds," but you aren't going to lose twenty pounds in a single day. Each day of your diet, you have to decide, "I'm going to stay on my diet today," and then you have to choose to eat the right things. Deciding once and for all is a necessary first step, but if that's all you do, you'll never lose the twenty pounds.

The same goes for following Me. I have given you control over your own life. You can hand that control back over to Me in trust and obedience, or you can keep that control and do things your own way. At any time today, you can choose not to obey Me. The battle for who's in charge of your life is a constant, 24/7 battle. It's always on. That's why every day (and several times during the day) you need to pray, "Lord, be in control of my life. Today is Your day." The more you do that, the easier it gets to trust Me. Hang in there, moment by moment, day by day. I am leading you into a great life.

Your Leader,
Jesus

Obey Each Day

Open
ALL DAY

LOGON>>

<TEEN> Father, is there a special time that's best for praying?

<GOD> I think it's a good idea to get up in the morning before your day starts and pray then. It starts things off right. It's also good to pray before U go to bed, thanking Me for the day and asking Me to speak to U while U sleep.

<TEEN> Cool.

<GOD> Actually, U can pray all day long. I am always here, and I am always listening. U can spend all day connected to Me. U don't ever have to break the connection.

Pray all the time.
1thessalonians.5:17.msg

Prayer is really a fancy word for connecting with Me. You may have a quiet time when you get alone, read the Bible, pray for people, and for the world. Praying out loud in church with a group is another kind of prayer. Laying hands on a sick person, praying, and trusting Me to heal him or her is yet another kind of prayer.

You can memorize a short prayer in the morning and then pray it in your heart all day long. It might be something like "Have Your way," "You are in control," "Be glorified," or "I can do all things through Christ who strengthens me." You don't have to pray it out loud, and you don't have to keep it in the front of your mind. Just keep it in your heart and loop it. Return to it throughout the day. You will be amazed at the comfort and strength prayer adds to your day.

Your Peace,
God

MY Ways

LOGON>>

<TEEN> Lord, I don't mean any disrespect, but why are there rules? Why can't people just do what they think is best?

<GOD> Well, what if you wanted to do something that hurt somebody else? Or what if somebody else wanted to do something that hurt you? It just wouldn't work out, because people don't always want the right things.

<TEEN> So you're saying that rules are there to help us?

<GOD> Totally! I wouldn't just make up a bunch of rules for no reason, and I certainly wouldn't do it just to be mean. Any rules I put in the Bible are there to make your life better, so check them out. The Ten Commandments are a good place to start.

Oh, how I love your law! I meditate on it all day long.
p s a l m . 1 1 9 : 9 7 . n i v

These days, few people appreciate the value of a good law. The majority seem to think it's cool to be a rebel and rules are meant to tie you down. But without laws and rules, fun would not be possible. How could you enjoy a game of football if there were no rules? Everyone would just run wild, and the game would fall apart. Anyone who thinks that anarchy is fun has never tried it. Anarchy means strong people abusing weak people. Nobody could save money, plant crops, or eat food, because lawlessness would prevail. Rules protect people.

If human laws can be good, just think about how perfect My laws are. King David actually celebrated them. He was partying because of My laws. Why? Because My laws are like the fence that keeps you from falling into a ditch. My laws are like the road that leads you to a better place. Learn to love My laws—and discover the perfect path to freedom.

Your Protector,
God

God's Laws
Set Us Free

Not Just
for Sundays

LOGON>>

`<TEEN>` God, I just got my feelings hurt in a major way, none of my work is finished, and everything I do seems to fall apart. I'm tired. I'm sick. It seems like my entire life is falling apart. Help me!

`<GOD>` Yes! That's what I like to hear.

`<TEEN>` What? U like to hear that I'm doing badly?

`<GOD>` No, I like that you're being honest with Me. Don't hold back. Bring all your pain to Me, and I will hear U out and give U hope.

I pour out my complaints before him
and tell him all my troubles.
For I am overwhelmed.
p s a l m . 1 4 2 : 2 - 3 . n l t

<<DOWNLOAD

You don't have to dress up in your Sunday best every time you want to talk to Me. You don't have to be all cheerful and smiley. I'm with you for the long haul. I want to hear the good, the bad, and the ugly. I can take it.

If your heart is breaking, if you are feeling weighed down, don't keep it to yourself. Just bring it all to Me. You don't even have to get it all together. Bring every single concern you have to Me. Pray them out loud one by one as they come to your mind. Cry. Yell. Get down on your face. Whatever you are feeling, share it with Me. I will share your pain, take it from you, and replace it with hope. I will hold you close and comfort you. I will give you hope for the future. Don't hold back. I'm here for you.

Your Comforter,
God

Come As YOU ARE

More Than
Meets the Eye

LOGON>>

<TEEN> I don't think others see me the way U see me. And I know I don't see them the way U do.

<GOD> That's true. U may only see them as dirty bums or annoying geeks, but those are just surface appearances. There is always something more going on underneath.

<TEEN> If I see what U see, will it make me sad?

<GOD> It may. My heart breaks for people all the time. But there are also things about people that make Me rejoice and sing.

"Man looks at the outward appearance,
but the Lord looks at the heart."

1samuel.16:7.niv

Things aren't always what they seem. The plumber may have a leaky pipe in his basement. The mechanic may have a broken car in his garage. People who seem as if they have it all together at church on Sunday may spend all week feeling depressed and defeated. You can see only the surface, but I see what's going on beneath the surface.

So when you pray for people, don't just pray about what you can see. Ask Me what I see, listen, and then pray what I tell you to pray. A lot of times you can see only the fruit of someone's problems, but I see the root. Even if you asked them, they might not be able to explain their problem. It's fine to start off praying for prayer requests that people have, but always take time to wait and hear what else I want you to pray. You are natural, but I am supernatural. I want to show you people's hearts so you can love them and pray for them in supernatural ways. I want you to see My miracles, and the first step is to see people through My eyes.

Your Vision,
God

See What God Sees

S.O.S.

LOGON>>

<TEEN> Jesus, where R U. I keep checking in, trying to talk to U, but U aren't there. Where R U? Have U left me alone down here? I feel alone. Will U answer me? R U there at all? How can I fix this? How can I reach U? What should I do? Jesus?

"I am with you always, even to the end of the age."
matthew.28:20.nkjv

Sometimes it feels as if I am not there, and it seems that no amount of praying can help you reach Me. One Christian described this experience as "the dark night of the soul." There is nothing worse than feeling like I have left you all alone. But you are not alone. I am here. Hang in there, keep praying, keep obeying Me, and you will experience My presence. Sin can separate you from Me. So if you're sinning, confess it to Me and turn from it.

On the Cross, I became sin for you. I took on your sin, and My Father turned His face away from Me in judgment. Up to that point in time, My Father and I had been together every moment of every day, but on the Cross He had to turn away. And I felt all the loneliness and abandonment that all humans have ever felt and ever will feel. So I know what it feels like to be forsaken. But you are not forsaken. My cross is the bridge between you and the Father; you never have to feel that kind of loneliness again. I am always with you.

Your Companion,
Jesus

God Is by Your Side

JESUS Has a Posse

LOGON>>

<TEEN> Jesus, what did U and Your friends talk about? U know, when U weren't driving out demons and preaching and stuff.

<JESUS> All sorts of things. They would ask Me questions about life. I'd ask them questions about who they thought God was. I'd tell them stories and show them things in nature.

<TEEN> Was it like Sunday school?

<JESUS> Actually, it was more like hanging out with your friends, just talking about life.

"Where two or three have gathered together in My name, I am there in their midst."
matthew.18:20.nasb

When I walked the earth, I met with My friends in small groups all the time. Some nights we'd hang out around a campfire on the lakeshore, eating fish and telling stories. Other times we'd get into deep conversations as we walked from town to town. I'm still the same way. I love meeting with people in small groups.

If there is a small group that you can join at your church, be a part of it. It may be a youth group or a group that meets regularly at someone's home. You may just want to get together with a group of Christian friends who go to your school. At the start of every meeting, pray and ask Me to be there with you as a part of your group to direct the conversation. Then you can read the Bible and talk about it, you can share your struggles and pray for each other, or you can just have fun hanging out. A group of close friends is a priceless thing. I want to be part of your group.

Your Friend,
Jesus

Hang Out with God's Friends

Heads UP

LOGON>>

<TEEN> Lord, I have all these problems and worries. There are
so many things on my plate to do. Is there any solution?

<GOD> Sure. Go help someone else who needs help.

<TEEN> I barely have time to do the things I need to do :-(
How is helping someone else going to change my situation?

<GOD> When U help others, U show My heart of kindness,
and it opens doors for Me to work more effectively in your own
life.

*Whenever you possibly can,
do good to those who need it.
Never tell your neighbors to wait until
tomorrow
if you can help them now.
proverbs.3:27-28.tev*

There is a bumper sticker that says, "Practice random kindness and senseless acts of beauty." Actually, I want you to practice purposeful kindness and intentional acts of beauty. Don't just be willing to help somebody, but go out of your way to look for someone to help. Before you start your day, pray and ask Me to lead you to someone who needs help. And then keep your eyes open throughout the day looking for that person.

You can get so caught up in your own life that you miss the needs of people around you. As My child, you represent Me to the world. Helping people can be simple—opening the door for someone who has their hands full, helping your parents around the house, listening to somebody's problems and praying with them. Time spent on other people is never wasted. Don't wait until tomorrow. Today is the day.

Your Helper,
God

Reach Out and Help

My House Is Your House

LOGON>>

<TEEN> God, is everything for U, or is it for us?

<GOD> A little of both. Everything that exists is mine, and I made it for My pleasure. There are creatures at the bottom of the ocean that no one will ever see but Me. There are stars and planets that no one may ever visit or even discover, but I get a kick out of them.

<TEEN> So it's all for U?

<GOD> Not at all. Every time U appreciate a sunset, My heart leaps. Every time someone discovers a new star, I smile. I made it to share with U.

Since you are his child, everything he has belongs to you.

galatians.4:7.nlt

In Mexico, they have a saying, "My house is your house." That's what I'm saying to you. You are My child. No room in My house is off limits to you. I may be the King of the universe, seated on a throne, but you are free to crawl up in My lap and lean into My chest. In the same way, the world you live in is My world, and I want you to enjoy it.

While you are on the earth, I will give you things to be responsible for—money, objects, vehicles, and many other things. Even more importantly, I will give you spiritual gifts—wisdom, understanding, love, creativity, strength, and endurance. I want to share all I have with you. Go outside and look at the sky, the trees, the stars at night, or even a single blade of grass. I made all these things for you to enjoy. And if you think the earth is beautiful, wait until you see Heaven! I want to share it all with you.
You are My precious child.

Your Papa,
God

You Have
Total Access

One God!
Fits All

LOGON>>

\<TEEN\> Jesus, sometimes it seems like U R just the God of church, not the God of the whole world.

  \<JESUS\> **I know! Sometimes I think Christians want to lock Me up in church so that they have to deal with Me only on Sundays! :-D**

  \<TEEN\> I think U R big enough to be the God of the whole world, and the God of my everyday life! U can handle all the stuff that happens in my life, right?

  \<JESUS\> **I made the universe. I endured the Cross. I raise people from the dead. I can help U with your daily struggles. And I want to ;-)**

My God will meet all your needs
according to his glorious riches
in Christ Jesus.
philippians.4:19.niv

<<DOWNLOAD

I made you, and I know what you need. I lived in the world. I under-stand about relationships, deadlines, pressures, and heartaches. None of those things are strange to Me. I want to help out with every area of your life. I have so much to give—joy, fun, fulfillment, security, wisdom, and guidance for practical, day-to-day living.

I am even fun enough to help you have a good time. Open the doors and include Me in more than just your "spiritual" life. I want to provide what you need in every area of your life.

Your Provider,
Jesus

God Is for All Times

LOVE WAITS

LOGON>>

<TEEN> God, will I ever get married?

<JESUS> I know the answer.

<TEEN> I know U know. Why won't U tell me?

<JESUS> I'll tell U when I'm ready for U to know.

<TEEN> So how does that help me now?

<JESUS> First I want U to learn how to let Me love U. I will use people in your life to show U My love. Loving Me and receiving My love helps U know better how to love others— including someone U might marry.

The LORD God said,
"It is not good for
the man to be alone.
I will make a helper suitable for him."
genesis.2:18.niv

I understand that you get lonely. I never married. It was just Me, My Heavenly Father, and My friends. Some people are created for marriage, and some people remain single. If you really want to get married, I want to give you the desires of your heart. So what do you do in the meantime?

Always be thinking about your future spouse. If you go on a date with somebody, will your future spouse be proud of your actions on that date, or will it make them sad? If it will make them sad, then don't do it. Until you marry somebody, you haven't really committed to that person (even if you've been dating for a long time and really like them). So don't have sex with them yet. There is plenty of time for sex and physical romance in marriage. Until then, bring your loneliness to Me. I will comfort you and give you the patience you need to wait.

Your Friend,
Jesus

Take Your Lonliness to God

Play Your Position

LOGON>>

<TEEN> Jesus, why did I get the short end of the stick?

<JESUS> What **R U** talking about?

<TEEN> It seems like everybody is so much more talented than I am. What am I good for?

<JESUS> **You're good for all sorts of amazing things. U greatly underestimate yourself.**

The way God designed our bodies is a model for understanding our lives together as a church: every part dependent on every other part.
1corinthians.12:25.msg

Do you ever look at someone else and wish you could be like them? Maybe they speak well, look great, are smart, or run fast. But ask yourself this—if that person is so great, then why didn't I make everybody like that? The reason is, I need different people to do different jobs. If everybody on a boat were the navigator, then nobody would be rowing. If everybody on a soccer team were the goalie, then nobody would be scoring goals.

This may sound crazy, but the Church is My "body" on earth. Now that My physical body is in Heaven, My Church is left to do the work. I am the head of this Church-body, and everybody else has a specific part to play in it. The Church is like a team. If everybody were a mouth, then nobody could hear. If everybody were an eye, then nobody could smell. I made you a certain way to fit into My Church. So don't try to be somebody else. Stop comparing yourself to other people. Look at yourself and see what you're good at; think about what you like to do. If you can't figure it out, pray and ask Me. I'll show you what you're good for.

Your Coach,
Jesus

Don't Underestimate YOU

Don't Be a Stranger

LOGON>>

<TEEN> It seems like sometimes UR the only one I can talk to about my problems.

<GOD> I am glad that U share your problems with Me, but sometimes it's good to talk to somebody with skin on.

<TEEN> What do U mean? Aren't U enough?

<GOD> Actually, no. I designed U to need other people. I want U to get to know and love each other. If U never share your problems with people, then UR missing out on one of the best things about My Church.

Share each other's troubles and problems,
and in this way obey the law of Christ.
galatians.6:2.nlt

Everybody's got problems, but not everybody shares them. There are a whole lot of pretenders in the world today. If you could see behind the smiles, fancy clothes, and boastful talk, you'd find a bunch of hurting people. There's nothing wrong with having problems. There is something wrong with keeping them to yourself.

I don't want you to be fake. I want you to be real. Definitely continue to share your problems with Me. But also take advantage of Christian friends who love you, and risk being vulnerable with them as well. Reach out; share your problems and ask for prayer. You don't have to tell your problems to everybody. In fact, you shouldn't. But you do need to share them with somebody you trust. It works both ways. You should also be willing to listen when people tell you their problems. You don't always have to have an answer for them. Just listen and pray with them. I will do the rest.

Your Counselor,
God

LET IT Go

LOGON>>

<TEEN> God, how can I forgive people when they have hurt me so much? I feel like I have a right to stay angry.

<GOD> I understand your feelings. Forgiveness doesn't mean that the other person is innocent. Forgiveness is choosing to release them anyway.

<TEEN> But I don't want to forgive. I feel like I can't.

<GOD> I will help U. I'm an expert at forgiveness. Remember, I'm the one who forgave U.

You must make allowance for each other's faults and forgive the person who offends you. Remember, the Lord forgave you, so you must forgive others.
colossians.3:13.nlt

If you ever need a reason to forgive somebody, think of My love and mercy toward you. You didn't earn Heaven, but I gave it to you. Your sin and disobedience made you My enemy, but I adopted you as My child. Heaven and My Spirit are all gifts that I've given to you, regardless of your past mistakes.

I want you to forgive other people in the same way. Forgiveness doesn't mean that you pretend it didn't happen. If somebody hits you in the face, pretending it didn't happen doesn't solve the problem. You realize that it happened, you realize that it's a problem, but you choose to let that person off the hook. You refuse to hold it against them. They are still accountable to Me for their actions. Forgiveness is not easy; it's a miracle. You can't do it without My help. But think about all I've done for you, all I've forgiven you, and this will make it easier to forgive other people.

Your Mercy,
God

FORGIVE

A True FRIEND

LOGON>>

<TEEN> Father, sometimes a little lie doesn't seem too wrong.

<GOD> Sin is sin—little or big.

<TEEN> But there are times when it feels like lying is the right thing to do.

<GOD> No. It's always best to tell the truth and trust Me to take care of the rest. U can still be tactful without being rude. But lying is never My way.

An honest answer is a sign of true friendship.

proverbs.24:26.tev

Suppose you are just about to go to a party with your friend, and you notice that his pants have a big rip right down the back. He turns to you and asks, "How do I look?" You could be nice and say, "Oh, you look great," but how does that help him? When he gets to the party, everybody is going to notice the rip and make fun of him. Then he'll turn to you and ask, "Why didn't you tell me the truth?"

Sometimes the truth is difficult to swallow. Sometimes the truth hurts people's feelings. Not everybody wants to hear the truth. But if you are going to be a good friend, a true friend, then you need to tell the truth. If all you do is tell people what they want to hear, then how will they ever change and get better? Please realize that there is a difference between telling the truth and just being rude. You don't ever want to tell the truth just to rub somebody's nose in something; you always want to tell the truth in love. Your friends might not thank you right away, but they will thank you eventually. They'll also trust you more, and you'll have better, closer friends.

The Truth,
God

U Don't Need the Spotlight

LOGON>>

<TEEN> Lord, this might sound conceited, but I feel like nobody knows how good I am.

<GOD> So, what does it matter?

<TEEN> Well, I want people to know.

<GOD> Don't worry about that. Just be yourself and do your best. I want U to show people how good I am, not how good U are. I want them to see Me through U.

Clothe yourselves with humility
toward one another, because,
"God opposes the proud
but gives grace to the humble."
1peter.5:5.niv

When you think about it, what does anybody have to brag about? Can you brag on what you made with your hands, or what you thought with your mind? Who made your hands? Who made your mind? Every breath you take, every beat of your heart is a free gift from Me.

So please, don't brag. It's embarrassing. When you meet someone who's bragging, don't get in there and argue with them about who's the best. Just let them brag. If I do anything good through you, and I want people to see it, then I will lift you up and promote you. It's much better to under-promote yourself than to over-promote yourself. Then people will be pleasantly surprised when they discover your hidden talents. Don't get Me wrong; if you are the right person for the job, then speak up and get in there and use your gifts for Me. If you're humble, I'll do the bragging for you. Trust Me.

Your Promoter,
God

Let God do Your Bragging

Keep It to Yourself

LOGON>>

\<TEEN\> How bad is gossip? Is it a big sin or a little sin?

\<GOD\> Sin is sin to Me. There is no little sin. And I particularly dislike gossip.

\<TEEN\> What's so bad about it?

\<GOD\> The person who gossips is looking for the limelight. Rather than defending another person's reputation, the gossiper uses information—fact or fiction—to bring themselves up in the eyes of others. But in the end, gossip always bites back.

*Gossip is spread
by wicked people;
they stir up trouble
and break up friendships.*
proverbs.16:28.tev

Gossip is sneaky and deceitful. There's nothing innocent or funny about gossip. Its purpose is to hurt. What if you came across one of your friends who was hurt and lying in a ditch? Instead of helping him out, you went and told another friend, "Oh, my gosh! He tripped and fell into a ditch! Can you believe it?" That's what gossip is like.

I want you to be a good friend, and I want you to have close friends. In order for that to happen, you have to prove yourself trustworthy. Nobody shares their heart with a gossiper. When you gossip to somebody, you're telling that person, "I'm not trustworthy. I'm the type of person who can't keep a secret." The next time they have something private to share, they'll know not to share it with you. When a friend shares something personal with you, keep it to yourself. And when somebody tries to share gossip with you, don't listen. Stop up your ears. Tell them, "I don't want to know anything about it." Gossip can't spread if people refuse to listen to it..

Your Close Friend,
God

Be a Good FRIEND

Like a Fish in Water

LOGON>>

<TEEN> What's so bad about skipping church?

<GOD> Why do U want to skip?

<TEEN> Sometimes church is just boring. Do U have to go to church to be a Christian?

<GOD> Do U have to swim in water to be a fish? :)

<TEEN> No. A fish is a fish in or out of water.

<GOD> Right. But a fish is going to have a pretty difficult time out of water, just like a Christian is going to have a pretty difficult time out of church.

*Let us not give up
the habit of meeting together,
as some are doing. Instead,
let us encourage one another.*
h e b r e w s . 1 0 : 2 5 . t e v

The same way I made a fish to need water, I made Christians to need each other. A local church is simply a group of Christians who admit that they need each other.

At church, you are encouraged, reminded of my goodness and faithfulness, you get to know other Christians, and you share your lives with one another. There is a commitment involved. When you join a church, you are telling the people at that church, "We're in this thing together. I'm here for you." There is no such thing as a perfect church, because there are no perfect people, and churches are made up of people. But you don't need a perfect church; you just need a church. If you don't already go to church on a regular basis, start going. My miracles happen in the middle of My people. Ask Me, and I'll show you what church I want you to be a part of.

Your Father,
God

KEEP
Friends

LOGON >>

<TEEN> Jesus, when U lived down here, did U have any close friends?

    <JESUS> U bet. I had twelve of them.

    <TEEN> Did U ever have a serious fight with any of them?

    <JESUS> One time My friend Peter denied that he knew Me. He turned his back on Me.

    <TEEN> What did U do?

    <JESUS> I forgave him, and then I went looking for him and made things right with him.

If you enter your place of worship and, about to make an offering, you suddenly remember a grudge a friend has against you, abandon your offering, leave immediately, go to this friend and make things right. Then and only then, come back and work things out with God.
matthew.5:23-24.msg

<<DOWNLOAD

I want you to be at peace with everybody. Maybe somebody is mad at you right now. You've asked them to forgive you, but they won't. That's not your problem. You can't make somebody forgive you. But what if somebody is mad at you and you haven't tried to make it right with them? That kind of relationship is like a splinter, always bothering you. I don't want you to be at odds with anybody if you can help it.

So right now, pray and ask Me to show you if there is anybody like that in your life. If somebody comes to mind, then go right now and call them. Don't wait until tomorrow. Set up a time to meet with them, write an e-mail—do whatever it takes. But let them know that you value their friendship. Maybe they are too mad or too hurt to take the first step. So you need to do it. You are not responsible for how they respond. But you have to try to make it right.

Your Peace,
Jesus

Always Make PEACE!

Plank-Eye Syndrome

LOGON>>

<TEEN> Jesus, am I good or bad compared to my friends?

<JESUS> Why do U ask?

<TEEN> Well, it seems like I'm doing pretty well compared to a lot of my friends.

<JESUS> But how do U know? I created U and each of your friends to be individuals. It's better not to compare yourself to other people.

"First get rid of the log from your own eye;
then perhaps you will see
well enough to deal with the speck
in your friend's eye."
matthew.7:5.nlt

It's much easier to criticize someone else's life than to improve your own life. Judging others is almost always a waste of time. If you spend time criticizing the decisions others make, that leaves less time to spend with Me, focusing on your own life. And if you ever catch yourself feeling glad about someone else's failure, that's a sure sign your heart is in the wrong place.

Whenever I allow you to see someone else's problems, it should break your heart. I don't show you these things so you can sit in judgment; I show you these things so you can help that person and feel the compassion of My heart for them. I am a just judge, and I will judge everyone fairly. Your job is to obey Me and to help people. A great place to start is to pray for them.

Your Just Judge,
 Jesus

Let God Be the JUDGE

Respond in
the Opposite Spirit

LOGON>>

<TEEN> Jesus, U got mad, right?

<JESUS> Definitely. Read about how I tore up the temple. I was furious.

<TEEN> So it's OK to be mad?

<JESUS> The Bible says to be angry but don't sin. When someone makes you angry, there is a right and wrong way to respond. U can't let your emotions control your actions.

A gentle response defuses anger,
but a sharp tongue kindles a temper-fire.

proverbs.15:1.msg

Have you ever sent a mean e-mail only to wish that you could take it back? Have you ever said an angry word in the heat of an argument that you didn't really mean? I want you to be in control of your temper. You can get angry. There's nothing wrong with that. But don't sin. Don't let your anger lead you to say or do something that you wish you hadn't.

Your tongue is a powerful thing. You can use words to build somebody up and calm them down. So learn how to control what you say. Slow down. Count to ten. Breathe deeply. Walk away. Pray. Wait. You don't have to answer people right away. Take some time. It's not just what you say, but how you say it. You could say the same thing in two different ways, and it could have two totally different outcomes. I don't want you to water down the truth. You can still speak the truth, but be wise about it. Respond in the opposite spirit. If somebody is coming at you all fired up, take it slow and answer them like ice water. It's more important to win friends than it is to win an argument.

Your Peace,
Jesus

Count to TEN

Come
CLOSER

LOGON>>

<TEEN> Sometimes I feel like U R far away.

<GOD> Well, our visits have become less frequent.

<TEEN> I guess it's been a while.

<GOD> I'm only a whisper away. I'm waiting to hear from U, any time of day or night.

Draw close to God, and
God will draw close to you.
james.4:8.nlt

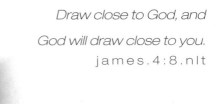

<<DOWNLOAD

If you feel like I'm far away from you, don't wait for Me to find you. Pray! Cry out to Me! Seek Me! Take time out of your day to sit still and listen for Me. I'm there, but sometimes there are things that cloud your heart that make it difficult for you to hear Me. Press through all the thoughts that call for your attention and focus on Me.

For every step you take toward Me, I'll take two steps toward you. I am just waiting for you to search for Me. Get involved in our relationship. If you look for Me with your whole heart, you will always find Me. I promise.

Your Friend,
God

PLANT Yourself

LOGON>>

<TEEN> Jesus, I still have the same temptations I've had
before. Sometimes I don't feel like I'm changing at all.
Sometimes it feels like I'm getting worse :-{

<JESUS> Don't be so quick to give up. U have good days,
and U have bad days; but if U keep following Me, it will all be
worth it.

<TEEN> I sometimes wonder, what's the point of reading the
Bible? What's the point of praying at all?

<JESUS> Don't get discouraged. Hang in there. U can't see
yourself changing, but I can. I can see the wonderful person
that UR becoming.

Let your roots grow down into [Christ]
and draw up nourishment from him.
See that you go on growing in the Lord,
and become strong and vigorous
in the truth.

colossians.2:7.tlb

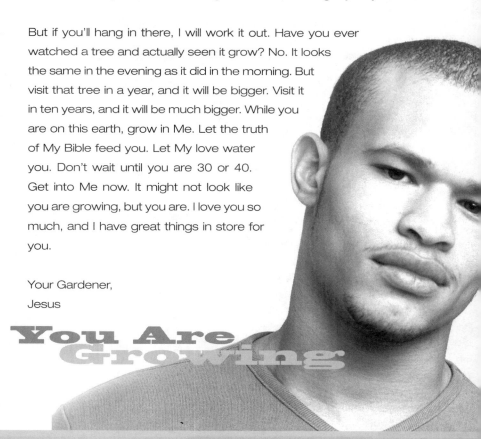

<<DOWNLOAD

Growing up is a gradual thing. Maybe you feel like things aren't changing fast enough. You still have problems; you still make the same mistakes; you still struggle with the same sins. Hang in there. Keep reading the Bible and connect with Me through prayer. Be patient. It took you awhile to develop bad habits, doubts, and fears. And it will take you some time to get used to following My ways.

But if you'll hang in there, I will work it out. Have you ever watched a tree and actually seen it grow? No. It looks the same in the evening as it did in the morning. But visit that tree in a year, and it will be bigger. Visit it in ten years, and it will be much bigger. While you are on this earth, grow in Me. Let the truth of My Bible feed you. Let My love water you. Don't wait until you are 30 or 40. Get into Me now. It might not look like you are growing, but you are. I love you so much, and I have great things in store for you.

Your Gardener,
Jesus

You Are Growing

Let Me Help

LOGON>>

<TEEN> Father, I feel like UR judging me. I feel like nothing is good enough for U. Can I ever live up to Your standards?

<GOD> Not without My help! And I want to help!

<TEEN> I'm glad to hear I don't have to do it all by myself.

<GOD> Lean on Me, and I'll show U a higher way.

God is working in you,
giving you the desire to obey him
and the power to do what pleases him.
philippians.2:13.nlt

Some think they are in a one-man play, and I am the audience. One false move, one wrong line, and I might stand up, boo, and start throwing tomatoes at them. Not at all! It's more like you are in the play, and I am your director. I tell you where to go. I help you learn your lines. If you forget your lines, I even whisper them to you. You are not on trial with Me. I am not waiting for you to fail. Actually, I'm doing everything I can to help you succeed.

Maybe you don't always want to follow Me. That's OK. Just be honest. Pray, "Lord, I don't want to follow You, but I want to want to follow You." I will meet you where you are and give you the desire to obey Me. You don't have to pretend you've got it all together. I'm not only your test-giver; I'm your tutor. I'm not only your judge; I'm your lawyer. Nobody wants you to succeed more than I.

Your Strength,
God

God Is on Your Side

Face-to-Face

LOGON>>

<TEEN> Jesus, I wish sometimes U were a real person.

<JESUS> I am a real person.

<TEEN> I know, I know. I mean I wish U were here, with a body and skin on.

<JESUS> I understand. My disciples knew Me like that when I lived on the earth. The good news is, you'll soon get to know Me in an even better way!

We can't even imagine what we will be like when Christ returns. But we do know that when he comes we will be like him, for we will see him as he really is.

1john.3:2.nlt

Heaven is an amazing place, and the most amazing thing about it is we'll be together! You won't have to imagine what I'm like. You won't have to guess at what I'm saying. You will actually hear My voice, see Me face-to-face, and know Me.

And you will be different too. Every day I am making you more and more like Me. But in Heaven, you really will be like Me. You won't sin anymore. You won't even want to. You will only want to hang out with Me, and I will only want to hang out with you. What a time we will have! Pure joy, relaxing peace, exciting adventures, great conversations, long walks, just time to hang out together. No more imagining and feeling distant. I will be right there with you forever. I can hardly wait.

The One Who Loves You Most,
Jesus

Look Forward

The Big Picture

LOGON>>

<TEEN> Jesus, sometimes I'm ashamed to stand up for U. I'm afraid people will make fun of me for being a Christian.

<GOD> Are those people more important than I am?

<TEEN> No.

<GOD> Then don't be afraid of them. In the big picture, what they think doesn't really matter.

<TEEN> Then help me see the big picture!

Since everything around us is going to melt away,
what holy, godly lives you should be living!
2peter.3:11.nlt

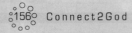

I want you to see things from My perspective. To you, it looks like physical things are solid and spiritual things aren't even there. But from My perspective, the physical things are like evaporating water, and the spiritual things are solid as a rock. You feel like you've got a long time to live on this planet. But I see your life as just a breath compared to the time you will spend in Heaven.

Have you ever had a dream, and then in the dream you realize you are dreaming? Suddenly, you can do anything—take risks, defy gravity, fight the bad guy, and become the hero. Why? Because you know the dream won't last and you will wake up safe and sound. From My perspective, your life on earth is like that dream. I am asking you to take risks. Live for Me. Obey Me. Love people. It doesn't matter what others think. In the end, the most important thing is your relationship with Me. Live your life with that in mind.

The Beginning and the End,
Jesus

Live For God

Simply OBEY

LOGON>>

<TEEN> Father, sometimes I wish U were my earthly father.

<GOD> Why?

<TEEN> Well, U understand everything I'm going through, but it seems like sometimes my parents just don't understand. They're not fair.

<GOD> They are the parents I gave to U, and if U want Me to help U out, U need to obey them.

Children, obey your parents in everything,
for this pleases the Lord.

colossians.3:20.niv

The Bible is pretty straightforward. Like when I say, "obey your parents," I mean "obey your parents." Maybe you think they are unfair. Maybe sometimes they actually are unfair. It's not your job to fix your parents. Your job is to obey them and pray for them. I am in charge of your parents, and they are responsible to Me.

I gave you to your parents for a reason. So don't always try to figure out what they are doing wrong. Your job is to obey them, even when you don't like their decisions. When you obey them, you are obeying Me. If you want Me to change their hearts, pray and ask Me to change their hearts. But they are never going to see your point if you are always disobeying them. Disobedience only hurts you. If you do your job and obey your parents, I can do mine and help you live the life I desire for you.

Your Father,
God

Obey Your Parents

Trading Places

LOGON>>

<TEEN> Jesus, remember on the cross when U said, "My God, why have U forsaken Me?"

<JESUS> How could I forget?

<TEEN> Did U just lose your faith? Or did God really abandon U?

<JESUS> My Father really abandoned Me. He turned his back on Me for the first time in all eternity. He was judging Me for your sins.

Christ was without sin,
but for our sake God made
him share our sin in order that
in union with him we might share
the righteousness of God.
2corinthians.5:21.tev

It's important that you understand what I did on the Cross—what it was all about. My crucifixion wasn't an accident. I could have come down from the Cross at any time. Instead, I chose to stay on the Cross because of you. While I was on the Cross, I was dying in your place, paying for your disobedience.

Think about it this way—two brothers are playing baseball in the front yard, and the younger brother intentionally throws the baseball right through their kitchen window. Glass shatters everywhere. Their father comes out and asks, "Who did this?" The older brother covers for the younger brother and says, "I'll take his punishment." So the older brother pays, and the younger brother goes free. The two swap places. I am like the older brother. I was innocent, but I took your punishment as if I were guilty. I took your place so you could go free, you could be forgiven, and I could help you choose the right thing. If you ever wonder how much I love you, just look at the Cross.

Your Sacrifice,
Jesus

Understand the Cross

Father and Child Reunion

LOGON>>

<TEEN> Father, why do we call U "Father?"

<GOD> Not everybody does. Just like not everybody on your street calls your earthly father "Dad." Only My children can call Me "Father."

<TEEN> What does it mean, then, that I am Your child?

<GOD> It means I love U wildly! I love U with a pride and a joy that is totally without bounds.

See how very much
our heavenly Father loves us,
for he allows us to be called his children,
and we really are!
1john.3:1.nlt

When I call you "My child," I'm not just saying that. You are actually My child. I could call you "servant," or "created being," or "follower," but I'd much rather call you "child." As your Heavenly Father, I don't imitate the relationship that you have with your earthly father. Actually, it's supposed to be the other way around. I created the father-child relationship on earth to help you understand the father-child relationship that we have. Our relationship is the original relationship. I am your true and everlasting father.

When I made you, I didn't want to know you as a servant, or even a friend. I wanted something much more intimate. I am here waiting for you to know Me as your loving Father. Jesus' death, burial, and resurrection restored your right to know Me this way. Don't keep Me at arm's length. Lean in to Me. Let Me hold you. If only you knew how much love I have for you! You are My precious, precious child. Let Me love on you.

Your Proud Father,
God

Let God
Love You

Fun, Inc.

LOGON>>

<TEEN> Father, do U like to have fun?

<GOD> I invented fun.

<TEEN> Really?

<GOD> I hold the patent :) However, there is a difference in what I consider fun and what others think of as fun.

A man can do nothing better than
to eat and drink and find satisfaction in his work.
This too, I see, is from the hand of God,
for without him, who can eat or find enjoyment?

ecclesiastes.2:24-25.niv

Some people think I'm a mean old stingy grump. *If I follow God,* they think, *He's going to take away all my toys and make me sit in the corner memorizing the entire book of Leviticus.* Many people fear I will keep all the good things to Myself and give them the leftovers. Nothing could be further from the truth.

I made all the good things on the earth, and I want to share them with you. When I say no to you, I'm only keeping you from harmful things so I can save you for the best things. I say no to sex outside of marriage, but I say an emphatic YES to sex within marriage. Sex in marriage is My idea! I say no to drugs, but I say an emphatic YES to music, hiking, friends, celebrating, good food, sunsets, sandy beaches, football, comedy—the list is practically endless. I want to share the wonders of My world with you. If I say no, it's not because I'm being stingy or holding back. It's because I've got something much better for you. Trust Me.

Your Loving Father,
God

Have Fun God's Way

It's All about LOVE

LOGON>>

<TEEN> Jesus, I know I'm supposed to want to love others, but there are certain people that I just hate.

  <JESUS> At least you're being honest. Have U ever prayed for them?

  <TEEN> No, not really. Do U think that would help?

  <JESUS> Definitely. I actually love those people. As U pray for them, My love starts flowing through U to them.

"Love your neighbor as yourself."

matthew.22:39.niv

As you read the Bible, if it seems that I often say some of the same things over and over again, it's because those things are important. I want you to understand what matters in life. I don't want you to waste your time on things that don't matter. You'll notice I didn't say, "Thou shalt go buy the most expensive pair of basketball shoes in your whole school." But I did say, "Love your neighbor as yourself."

You can memorize the Ten Commandments to learn what love is supposed to look like, but the power to actually love comes from Me. The more you let Me be in charge of your life, the more love you will have for other people. It will come naturally. You'll want to love. If you feel angry, selfish, or bitter toward someone, pray and ask Me to help you love them. The good news is, I already love them Myself (I love everybody), and I want to help you see them as I do. The more I'm in you, the more loving you will be.

Your Power,
Jesus

Don't Strut

LOGON>>

<TEEN> Jesus, my life was going so well that I put off reading my Bible and hanging out with U. Then the next thing I knew, everything started falling apart!

<JESUS> That's usually the way it happens.

<TEEN> Why? Why do I have to come back to U every day?

<JESUS> Well . . . :) I love U, and UR doing great, but U have a need to spend time with Me. Time with Me strengthens U and helps U stay on the path I've planned for your life.

Don't be so naive and self-confident.

You're not exempt.

You could fall flat on your face as easily as anyone else.

Forget about self-confidence; it's useless.

Cultivate God-confidence.

1corinthians.10:12.msg

How can you be confident without being proud? It's definitely a fine line to walk. The Bible says you can do all things through Me, but it also says that apart from Me you can do nothing. I don't want you strutting like a peacock, but I don't want you groveling around like some insect either. There is a middle ground. The solution to this problem requires two things—knowing yourself and knowing Me.

If you're honest with yourself, you'll see that you are capable of some pretty selfish, ugly things. So never think more of yourself than you should. It's okay to depend on Me—I want you to. As a matter of fact, just when you feel like you've gotten where you are all by yourself, that's usually when you fall. The Bible actually warns that pride comes before a fall. So when you least expect it, expect it. At the same time, realize that I live inside you, and I will never fail you. Be confident, but be confident in Me. You can't do it alone.

Your Strength,
Jesus

Be Confident in God

Change Your Scene

LOGON>>

<TEEN> I'm depressed.

<GOD> Is it anything in particular. Did anything bad happen?

<TEEN> It's nothing in particular. It's just . . . I think my friends are kind of bringing me down.

<GOD> Well, there's no rule that says U have to hang out with them, right?

<TEEN> Well, don't U want me to love everybody?

<GOD> Sure, but loving people doesn't mean becoming best friends with those who bring U down.

Run from anything that
gives you the evil thoughts . . .
but stay close to anything that
makes you want to do right.
2timothy.2:22.tlb

Your environment has a powerful effect on you—for good or bad. If you sit inside a black room all day long, you will lean toward depression. If you hang out with negative, cynical people who are always criticizing everything, you will become influenced toward doubt and bitterness. If you hang out with people who encourage you, you will grow in hope.

You can't always control your environment, but whenever you can, you should. Don't listen to music that makes you depressed. Don't watch movies that make you fearful. Don't hang out with people who put you down. Feed your soul and your spirit with beauty and truth. Read My Bible. Hang out with people who believe in Me and encourage your faith. Listen to music that inspires you. Don't let your environment bring you down. Change your environment so that it lifts you up. If you are in a really bad situation that you feel you can't change, ask Me to help bring you out of it. I will either bring you out, or I will give you the strength to deal with it. You do your part to change, and I will do the rest.

Your Encourager,
God

Feed Your SOUL

The Word
of God

LOGON>>

<TEEN> Jesus, will U ever tell me something that's not in the Bible?

<JESUS> Sure. But I'll never tell U something that goes against the Bible.

<TEEN> So U agree with the Bible 100 percent?

<JESUS> Always. When I was on earth, I obeyed it to the letter. It is the truth.

All Scripture is God-breathed and is useful for teaching, rebuking, correcting and training in righteousness, so that the man of God may be thoroughly equipped for every good work.

2timothy.3:16-17.niv

You are living in a world where people believe all sorts of wrong things. For instance, people will tell you that the Bible is full of mistakes, that it contradicts itself, that it is invented by men, that it's not trustworthy. But read what the Bible says about itself: "All scripture is God-breathed and useful." The Bible is My word to all men. No person made it up. I created it and helped people write it down.

The purpose of the Bible is to teach, rebuke, correct, and train—and that's just the short list. I want you to make the Bible the foundation of what you believe and how you think about the world. If somebody teaches something in school or church that seems weird, check it with the Bible. If you want to know Me—My personality, My opinions, My plans—read the Bible. Get to know it well. It is your direction to follow for a successful life with Me.

The Word,
Jesus

Know the BIBLE

A Matter
of Time

LOGON>>

<TEEN> Father, school is driving me crazy!

<GOD> I can see that :) How can I help?

<TEEN> Get me out of school? Maybe?

<GOD> Not possible. Now is the season for U to be in school.
But U won't be in school forever.

Everything on earth has its

own time and its own season.

ecclesiastes.3:1.cev

There are some things that are absolutely right or wrong. You're never going to wake up one morning and suddenly it's OK to lie. It will always be wrong to lie. Then there are other things that are simply a matter of timing. Leaves don't fall in the summer. It's not wrong for leaves to fall; it's just that summer is not the season for it.

Your life is the same way. It has seasons: youth, adulthood, middle age, old age, death, and eternity. You are not going to accomplish everything I have planned for you in a single season. One day you will be ready for adulthood, but it's not time yet. You have to wait. Fortunately, I have given you plenty of things to do now. In this moment, school is in season for you. Obeying parents and guardians is in season for you. So use this season of your life to do the things I've given you to do, and do them well. Pay attention, study up, and obey. There will come a season when you are the teacher, the leader, or even the parent. There will even come a season where you're body grows old and you aren't able to do the things you can do now. So enjoy your youth, and be patient.

Your Creator,
God

Guard Your Eyes

LOGON>>

<TEEN> Father, is it OK to talk about sex with U?

<GOD> Of course. I know what you're thinking anyway, remember?

<TEEN> Ouch! OK, Lord, sometimes I have sexual fantasies. I've seen pictures I shouldn't have seen.

<GOD> Lust is definitely a sin, but it's not as rare as everyone pretends. Confess it and turn from it. Lust often starts with your eyes, so get control of what U watch.

I made a covenant with my eyes
not to look with lust upon a young woman.

job.31:1.nlt

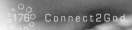

There is a difference between simply admiring the beauty of someone and lusting after them. What's the difference between a nude painting and pornography? It is determined by the attitude of your heart. Are you looking at that person wanting to bless them, or are you looking at them wanting to use them? Lust uses people, even if it only happens in your mind. Even worse, lust hurts you. Once you take a lustful image in through your eyes, it begins to eat away at your heart. A lustful image has a life of its own.

If you've already looked at pornography, if you've already looked lustfully at someone, then you need to get those images out of your mind and heart. Confess it as sin, and ask Me to remove those images from you. Then, make a deal with your eyes. The next time you are tempted to look lustfully at someone (on the Internet, in class, at the mall), turn your eyes away. Look at something else. If you can, get up and walk away. Lustful images can rot you from the inside out. So don't let them inside. You are the boss of your eyes, and your eyes are the windows to your soul. Connect with Me, and I'll help you focus your eyes on pure things.

Your Filter,
God

Control Your Eyes

Trials Come,
Trials Go.

LOGON >>

<TEEN> Jesus, will following U make my life better?

<JESUS> Definitely.

<TEEN> Then why do I still have challenges? Why do things still turn out bad sometimes? What's wrong?

<JESUS> Nothing is wrong. It's just that sometimes life is tough.

*Don't be bewildered or surprised
when you go through
the fiery trials ahead,
for this is no strange, unusual thing
that is going to happen to you.*
1peter.4:12.tlb

Sometimes things have to get worse before they get better. Think about it in terms of cooking: In order to make a delicious meal, you have to dirty some dishes first. Halfway through the cooking process, the average kitchen looks like a construction zone for food. But in the end, the meal comes together, the mess is cleaned up, guests are fed, and everything is better than before.

In your life, the same is true. The Christian life is full of trials. But I promise to get you through the trials. Plus, I will give you peace and joy in the middle of the trials. I will carry your burden. I will walk beside you and hold you up. Trials are a normal part of the Christian life, so hang in there. We'll get through it, and you'll be better because of it. The benefit of being a Christian is knowing you can always count on Me.

Your Strength,
Jesus

Endure Life's Challenges

close to U

LOGON>>

<TEEN> Jesus, please help me.

<JESUS> I'm here.

<TEEN> Please help me. I need U to be near to me. I'm not making any excuses. I don't know what else to pray. Please help me.

<JESUS> I understand. I'm right there with U now. I'm not going anywhere. I will rescue U.

The LORD is close to the brokenhearted;
he rescues those who are crushed in spirit.

psalm.34:18.nlt

When you really hit the bottom, when you're at the end of your rope, when you have no other hope, that's when I'm there the most. I'm always with you, but when you are down and you have nowhere else to turn, that's when you reach out to Me. And you will always find Me. You need to understand that when your heart is breaking, mine is too. I feel the pain that you are feeling, and I reach out to comfort you.

The truth is, you live in a crazy, messed-up world with all sorts of evil happening all around you. I am compassionate—all-powerful, all-seeing, and all-knowing. Lean on Me. I am with you, and I hear you. I will come to your rescue. I am working on your behalf even when you can't see the results immediately. Trust Me.

Your Savior,
Jesus

Lean On JESUS

Your Life:
My Masterpiece

LOGON>>

<TEEN> Jesus, it seems like sometimes my life is so off track that U could never use me to do any good.

<JESUS> No way! I will never give up on U.

<TEEN> Between the sin that I do and the sin done to me, if I were U, I might give up on me.

<JESUS> But you're not me! I'll take the things U think are broken beyond repair, and I'll make something beautiful out of them. All U have to do is bring them to Me.

*We know that God
causes everything to work together
for the good of those who love God
and are called according
to his purpose for them.*
romans.8:28.nlt

Sometimes you mess your own life up by making wrong decisions, disobeying Me, being selfish, or whatever. Guess what? I can take even the messes you've made and work them for good. You don't have to be perfect or innocent in order for Me to make good things out of your life. You just have to confess your wrong and turn from it. Then we start over, right from where you are. One of My titles is "redeemer." That means I take messed-up situations and make them good. You are never so far off track that I can't start from where you are and make something good out of it. You have never blown it beyond repair.

Sometimes things happen to you, and they aren't your fault at all. I can even repair those situations and make something good out of them. When you love Me and say yes to Me, I turn your life into a work of art. And I'm a master of improvisation; I'm great at taking the unexpected and using it for good. Actually, nothing is unexpected to Me. So don't despair. Instead pray, and look for Me to do My work.

Your Redeemer,
Jesus

Hang On to Hope

Right on Time

LOGON>>

<TEEN> Lord, how come things change so slowly?

<GOD> "Slow" and "fast" are relative terms. What seems slow to U might be right on time to Me.

<TEEN> Then how can I see time from Your perspective?

<GOD> It all has to do with patience and trust. If you trust Me, then you will wait patiently for Me to do My work. I'm never late; it's just that some things take time.

These things I plan won't happen right away.
Slowly, steadily, surely, the time approaches
when the vision will be fulfilled. If it seems slow,
do not despair, for these things will
surely come to pass. Just be patient!
They will not be overdue a single day!

habakkuk.2:3.tlb

One good thing about Me is that I can't lie. So if I promise something is going to happen, you can be sure it will. One thing that can be frustrating for you about Me is that My timetable is different from yours. I don't live in time. I live outside of time. I created time. So I'm in the past, the future, and the present all at the same time. A thousand years is no time at all for Me. But a thousand years is like ten lifetimes for you. You and I see time differently.

You can trust Me. My timing is always perfect, but sometimes you have to wait. You can wait anxiously or you can wait patiently. Waiting anxiously means waiting with fear and impatience because you doubt it will happen. Waiting patiently means waiting with hope and excitement because you trust it will happen. I have great plans for you in My own timing. Just believe.

The Beginning and the End,
God

Trust God's Timing

 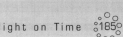

Pray For Mercy

LOGON >>

<TEEN> Father, I watch the news, and I get discouraged. Politicians lie. Corporations pollute and exploit. There is violence, drug abuse, divorce, and racism.

<GOD> I see it too.

<TEEN> What can I do about it? How can I make a difference?

<GOD> The first step is simply to obey Me and do things My way. The next step is to pray and ask Me to change your world.

If my people, who are called by my name, will humble themselves and pray and seek my face and turn from their wicked ways, then will I hear from heaven and will forgive their sin and will heal their land.

2chronicles.7:14.niv

If there are things wrong with the world around you (and we both know that there are), it's up to you to pray. When you see violence at your school, in your neighborhood, or in your nation, then pray and ask Me to change things.

Every country in the world has their own problems, but My people are praying to Me, crying out for Me to have mercy on their country. And I hear their prayers and answer them. In order for you to be part of the solution, refuse to be part of the problem. Be different. And when you pray, don't pray for My judgment. Pray for My mercy. Be humble, not proud. Ask forgiveness for your country. You have the power to change your world, and it starts with prayer.

The Ruler of Nations,
I AM

Change Your World

Send
Them Packing

LOGON>>

<TEEN> Jesus, what's the solution to temptation? It seems like I'm tempted to do the same wrong thing over and over again.

<JESUS> Have U tried saying no to the temptation?

<TEEN> A few times. But it keeps coming back. I'm eventually going to give in at some point, so why fight it?

<JESUS> U can't think that way. Don't give in. Keep resisting. Eventually, the temptation will bother U less and less. It does get easier, but U have to continue to resist.

Happy is the man who doesn't give in
and do wrong when he is tempted,
for afterwards he will get as his
reward the crown of life that God
has promised those who love him.
james.1:12.tlb

Temptation is a given. I was tempted when I lived on earth, and I was perfect. So it's a guarantee that you will be tempted. If you give in, temptation wins. As long as you continue giving in to the same temptation, it will keep coming back. Temptation is like an unwanted guest. He knocks on your door and asks to come in. "OK," you say, "but this is the last time. I don't want you coming around here anymore after this." Guess who'll be right back at your door tomorrow? You have to turn temptation away at the door. Send him packing. You'll probably have to do it several times before he gets the hint. But eventually, that temptation will come around less and less.

I can help you. I have already defeated all temptation. I never gave in to it, not once. And I live inside you to help you be strong. When temptation knocks on your door, send Me to answer it. Speak what the Bible says about it like I did: *It is written . . .* When you are tempted, immediately pray and ask Me to deliver you. Keep praying until I do. Eventually, freedom will be yours.

Your Guardian,
Jesus

Turn from Temptation

Stay Alert

LOGON>>

  <TEEN> What's the deal with the devil? Is he real or what?

  <GOD> Yes. He's real all right.

  <TEEN> What's he like? What does he do?

  <GOD> He's a liar. He steals, kills, and destroys. Most importantly, he's My defeated foe. U can think of him as a worm crushed under My shoe.

Stay alert.
The Devil is poised to pounce,
and would like nothing better
than to catch you napping.
1peter.5:8.msg

The devil wants you to think he is some guy in red tights with a pitch-fork and horns. If you think of him as a fairy tale or a myth, you won't be watching out for him. Now I don't want you to focus on Satan. He doesn't deserve that kind of attention. But I do want you to be alert. Understand that the devil wants to kill you, to steal your joy, and to destroy your relationship with Me. He and his demon thugs hate me, and they hate My children.

I want you to do what the Bible says, "Be wise about what is good, and innocent about what is evil. The God of peace will soon crush Satan under your feet" (Romans 16:19-20 NIV). In other words, you don't try to hunt Satan down and put him in a cage. I am the One who puts him under your feet. Your job is to do what is right and stay away from evil. Evil is a trap to mess you up and ruin your life. So don't slack off and give in to evil. Stay alert.

Watching with you,
God

Your Source

LOGON>>

  <TEEN> Everyone around me has an expectation of who they think I should be.

   <GOD> I have great expectations too.

   <TEEN> Sometimes I am not sure I want to be who they say I am.

   <GOD> Your identity is in Me. I know your purpose, and I'll show U.

"Your hands shaped me and made me."
job.10:8.niv

Nobody knows you better than I. I was intimately involved in your creation. I decided what you would look like, what you would be good at, even how long you will live. I didn't just make your body; I made your soul. I created you to be unique. I know you better than you know yourself.

With that in mind, don't let other people try to tell you who you are. Only I can tell you who you are. If I say you're wonderful and precious (and I do), then that's who you are. If I say you can do it, then you can do it. You are not an accident. You didn't just come into existence randomly. Don't you dare believe it. From the beginning of time, I knew that you would be born. I planned it out. I chose your parents. I even chose the era in which you would live. So listen to Me and let Me define you. Learn about yourself from Me. I want you to grow into the person I made you to be, and I'm the only one who can tell you who that is. I am your creator. If you're searching for who you are, look to Me. I am your source.

Your Maker,
God

Let God
Define You

 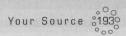

Good Work

LOGON>>

<TEEN> Jesus, is there such a thing as a non-Christian job?

<GOD> If U were a drug dealer or a bank robber, I'd say those would be non-Christian jobs :)

<TEEN> I mean regular jobs, like a dentist or a construction worker.

<GOD> The occupation U choose doesn't make U a Christian; instead, your relationship with Me should help U do better at your job.

Whatever you do, do it all for the glory of God.

1corinthians.10:31.niv

There are very few "unspiritual" jobs. I've used teachers, kings, shepherds, farmers, metal workers, tent-makers, musicians, and even priests to do My work. When I lived on earth, I Myself worked as a carpenter for years.

Auto mechanics, bakers, interior designers, architects, waiters—these are all "spiritual" professions if the person has a personal relationship with Me. As long as you do an honest day's work and you love those around you, then I can use your life to touch others. So don't give up your dream to be a ballet dancer, a race car driver, or a poet. You don't have to be a missionary in Africa to serve Me. Keeping Me at the center of your focus and your success—no matter where I lead you to work— will bring great rewards.

Your Coworker,
Jesus

Work For GOD

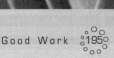

Share the Love

LOGON>>

<TEEN> Jesus, I feel like I know U better than I used to. Thanks for letting me get to know U.

<JESUS> My pleasure. I love getting to know U too. Can I ask a favor of U?

<TEEN> Sure. Anything.

<JESUS> I want U to tell others what I'm like.

<TEEN> Everybody?

<JESUS> No, no. That would take a while. Just the ones I show U.

If you teach these things to other followers,
you will be a good servant
of Christ Jesus.

1timothy.4:6.cev

"Discipleship" is a fancy word, but it's really pretty simple. It just means passing on what you know to someone else. Let that person hang out with you. Let them watch how you live and learn from you. I want you to share My love with people who don't know Me, and encourage those who do know Me by telling them about the great things we've done together.

Don't worry about trying to tell everybody. I will bring people into your life who will be interested in what you have to say. When this happens, tell them what you know about Me. Tell them that I'm a God of love. Tell them that I want to hang out with them and be real to them. Let them know how special they are to Me. I'm glad you know Me the way you do. I want other people to know Me too, and you are a mirror reflecting My love and goodness. Share it.

Your Teacher,
Jesus

Plan on Me

LOGON>>

<TEEN> Lord, does trusting U mean I should never make any plans?

<GOD> Not at all. It just means that U make Me a part of your plans. It means U stay flexible.

<TEEN> Give me an example.

<GOD> OK. U don't just get into a car and wait for it to take U somewhere. U have to know the direction U want to go. U start the car and head that way. Just be ready along the way for Me to change your course.

Many are the plans in a man's heart, but it is the LORD's purpose that prevails.

proverbs.19:21.niv

I want you to be wise, and I want you to plan for the future, but don't forget to make Me a part of your plans. There is a parable in the Bible about a man who spent his money on a big barn to store all his wealth. Just when he finished the barn, he died. Now I could have told him not to waste his time on that stupid barn, but he wasn't listening to Me. So don't assume I always want you to do something bigger and better. That's not always the case. But don't assume I want you to sit around doing nothing either. The Bible says, "If a man will not work, he shall not eat" (2 Thessalonians 3:10 NIV). You need to plan for your future, but plan with Me.

When it comes to the future, I want to be included. Don't make up your own plans and ask Me to bless them, but instead be flexible to adjust your course when I ask you to. Before you decide to go to a college, take a job, or finalize any major decision, pray and ask Me what I want. I have the best plans for your life, and I want to share them with you. Work with Me; involve Me in your details. Often the result will be far better than you imagined.

Your Counselor,
God

Make Plans with God

Home
Sweet Home

LOGON>>

<TEEN> Jesus, I feel like I'm really getting to know U better.

<JESUS> I feel the same way. I already know everything about U, but now I am getting to be your friend.

<TEEN> I wish U were really here on earth. Then I could invite U over to my house and we could hang out in person.

<JESUS> It will be like that in Heaven. Until then, know that I am real, and U can make a place for Me in your heart.

I pray that Christ will be more and more at home in your hearts.
ephesians.3:17.nlt

<<DOWNLOAD

The reason I saved you, the reason I went to the Cross, the reason you were created in the first place, was so we could get to know each other well. Our relationship is actually the main reason that you exist. Now that you know Me as your friend, I want us to be closer and closer.

Every new relationship starts off slowly. First, you meet someone. Then maybe you go out with them and a group of friends. Next, you see them one on one. Then, you invite them over to your house. Finally, they start coming over to see you more and more. The more you get to know them, the more at home they feel around you. It's the same with me, except I make My home in your heart. Ask yourself if I am in your heart as an occasional visitor, a weekend guest, or a close friend. I want to be your best friend. Keep hanging out with Me, and we will get to know each other better. I'm looking forward to it.

Your Friend,
Jesus

Hang with GOD

Stand Firm
Stand Strong

LOGON>>

<TEEN> Jesus, sometimes when I'm around a group of friends and they're making fun of somebody, it's easy for me just to go along with them, but I always feel bad about it later.

<JESUS> Have U ever tried standing up to them.

<TEEN> It's hard. I'm always afraid I'll seem like a goody-goody.

<JESUS> I understand, and I can help.

Our purpose is to please God, not people.

1thessalonians.2:4.nlt

202 Connect2God

There's nothing easy about peer pressure. When you are surrounded by a bunch of friends who are doing the wrong thing, it's hard to go against them and choose the right thing, especially if you are the only one who feels that way. In World War II, lots of Germans went along with Hitler not because they agreed with him, but because that's what everybody else was doing. Even when I was arrested, My good friend Peter denied he knew Me because he was surrounded by a bunch of people who were against Me, and he was afraid to stand up to them. Later, Peter was ashamed of his decision.

When all your friends are pressuring you to do the wrong thing, and it feels as if you are all alone, remember that I am there with you. You aren't alone. I am watching, pulling for you, helping you do what's right. Pretend that you are on a stage, and there is only one person in the audience—Me. In eternity, in Heaven, it won't matter what your friends thought of you. My opinion will be the only opinion that matters. So live to please Me, and you will find it much easier to choose the right thing.

Your Fan,
Jesus

Live to Please God

Your Generation
Is My
Generation

LOGON>>

<TEEN> Father, when will I have an opportunity to make a difference?

<GOD> U can make a difference right now.

<TEEN> It just seems like the focus is on the adult generation and what they can do.

<GOD> I don't think like that at all. I believe in U. I see so much strength and beauty when I look at your generation. I have a master plan for the world, and your generation plays a major part.

David . . . served the purpose of God
in his own generation
acts.13:36.nasb

<<DOWNLOAD

There is a reason you were born when you were born. I put you in the middle of your generation on purpose. I have a plan for you. You can't change the world of the past, and you can't directly change the world of the future, but you can change the world of the present, the world of your generation. I know you—I know your music, your style, and your culture.

Someone older may not be able to reach your friends with My love. You have to reach your friends; they will want to hear about Me from you. Don't assume that older people are always going to represent Me. In just a little while, your generation will be the older generation. I am looking for young Christians who will stand up for Me and share Me with the world around them. Will you accept the challenge? Will you fulfill My purpose for you in your own generation? Don't fear. You can do it. As a matter of fact, you're just the one for the job.

Your Leader,
God

Stand Up
for God

Raise Your Voice

LOGON>>

\<TEEN\> Sometimes I want to sing out loud and just celebrate U, but . . .

   \<GOD\> But what?

   \<TEEN\> Well, I'm not exactly the best singer :-(

   \<GOD\> R U kidding? Your voice sounds beautiful to Me. I can hear the love and praise coming from your heart. Don't ever be ashamed to sing to Me. U have every right, and I love it!

Praise him with the sounding of the trumpet,
praise him with the harp and lyre,
praise him with tambourine and dancing,
praise him with the strings and flute,
praise him with the clash of cymbals,
praise him with resounding cymbals.
Let everything that has breath praise the LORD.

psalm.150:3-6.niv

There are a million different ways to worship Me. Whether you worship Me with dancing, quiet music, or loud noisy music—the important thing is that you worship Me. Put your heart into it. Give it everything you've got. I've given you breath and life. I've given you a voice, so use it to praise Me.

Every sunset praises Me. Every mountain range shouts My praise. The huge oceans echo with praise for Me. All creation displays My glory. It shouts out, "Look how great God is!" So join in the praise. It doesn't matter whether or not you are musical. It doesn't matter how well you think you can sing. Raise your voice anyway. Raise your hands. If you're an artist, paint pictures. If you're a writer, write songs and poems. Get creative! Get emotional! Get passionate! Don't be ashamed. I want you to be enthusiastic and energetic about Me. Don't let the angels and the mountains out-praise you. Raise your voice!

The Almighty,
God

Give It Your All

Beauty for Ashes

LOGON>>

<TEEN> Jesus, I have all this crud in my heart that's bringing me down. Sadness, pain, bad memories.

<JESUS> I understand. But remember that I went to the Cross so U wouldn't have to carry all that stuff around.

<TEEN> So what do I do with it?

<JESUS> Bring it to Me. I am like a giant sponge that soaks up your pain. Give it all to Me. I can take it. And I will give U something beautiful in return.

God sent me to . . . comfort all who mourn,
To . . . give them bouquets of roses instead of ashes,
Messages of joy instead of news of doom.

isaiah.61:2-3.msg

You've heard of the Terminator? Well, I'm the Transformer. I change things. I take ashes and change them into beauty. I take sorrow and change it into joy. In My hands bad news turns to good news. Just think about the end of My life on earth. In just three short days it went from a depressing funeral to a resurrection celebration. When I was crucified, My followers felt like it was the end of the world; but when I rose from the grave, they felt that they could take on the world, and they did.

I want to transform your life if you'll let Me. Bring Me your ashes, your pain, all the things in your life that hurt and that you want to forget. Leave them at My feet. Just lay them down and ask Me to take them from you. I will begin healing you, replacing your pain with joy, giving you hope instead of fear. It's miraculous. You don't have to understand it. Just allow Me to do it. I'm here to comfort you, to heal the deepest pain in your heart. I love you so much, and I aim to make things right in your life. Open up your heart to Me and let Me fill it with everything I am.

Your Transformer,
Jesus

Open Your HEART

Coming Soon

LOGON>>

<TEEN> Jesus, when R U coming back to earth? U said U would, but it's been a long time.

  <JESUS> It won't be long now. I rose from the dead a mere 2,000 years ago. So U won't have to wait long.

  <TEEN> Will it happen in my lifetime?

  <JESUS> I don't know. Only the Father knows. But I guarantee it's going to happen.

"Yes, I'm on my way! I'll be there soon!
I'm bringing my payroll with me.
I'll pay all people in full for their life's work.
I'm A to Z, the First and the Final,
Beginning and Conclusion."
revelation.22:12-13.msg

I was born as a baby in a stable, and I died as a 33-year-old man on a cross. But the story didn't end there. I came back to life, went back to Heaven, and I'm coming back to earth again soon. This time I'm not coming as a baby. I'm coming as a victorious king on a white horse. My hair will be snowy white, and My eyes will be burning fire. I'm coming to make all things new—a new Heaven, a new earth, and a new life for us forever.

I'm also coming to judge and set things right. If things seem unfair or out of control in the world right now, I agree. They are. But that won't last forever. As sure as your heart is beating right now, I am on My way back to earth to set things right. So don't despair when you see evil. Don't lose heart. Don't give in. Hang in there and do what's right. Pray. Hope. Believe that I can change things. I'll see you soon.

The Beginning and the End,
Jesus

My Voice

LOGON>>

TEEN> Father, how do I learn to hear U?

<GOD> First, read the Bible and get to know what I'm like.

<TEEN> Then?

<GOD> Then be still, listen, and believe that I actually want to speak to U. I do.

Then God came and
stood before him exactly
as before, calling out,
"Samuel! Samuel!" Samuel answered,
"Speak. I'm your servant, ready to listen."
1samuel.3:10.msg

I want to speak to you more than you know. A great way to start hearing Me is to read the Bible. It is a clear, solid record of who I am. Learn about the things I did, the way I treated people, and the things I said. The best way to know Me is to know My Son, Jesus. Read the Gospels to learn about Him. By reading the Bible, you tune your ear to recognize the sound of My voice. You probably won't hear Me with your ears. You'll hear Me in your heart.

I want to speak to you personally. So after you read the Bible, be quiet and ask Me to speak to you. Just write down what you think I'm saying. You don't have to show it to anybody or prove it scientifically. That's not the point. At first, you may hear all sorts of things—some from me, some from yourself, some from the world around you. Practice listening. If you feel like I'm telling you to do something, try it out and see how it works. Be careful! I will never tell you anything that goes against the Bible. But I am alive. I am real. I am a person with a personality. And I still speak to My children. I want to speak to you, and you can learn to hear Me.

Your Counselor,
God

Practice Listening

Love
Lasts

LOGON>>

  <TEEN> Father, I feel like I'm wasting my time.

  <GOD> How do U mean?

  <TEEN> Well, I have all this work to do, but my friend called and wanted to talk about all her problems, so I wasted all my time just listening and trying to encourage her.

  <GOD> Listen, I understand about your work. Ask Me, and I'll help U get it done. But U did the right thing. Listening to someone's problems is an act of love, and love is never a waste of time.

These three things continue forever:
faith, hope, and love.
And the greatest of these is love.
1corinthians.13:13.ncv

<<DOWNLOAD

Few things on earth will last. The body you have now will not last. The things you own will deteriorate. Even the earth itself is going to be replaced by a new one. I know it's easy to become distracted by the things you want and the jobs you have to do. But concentrate on the things that are going to last forever.

Have faith—believe in Me and trust Me; let Me be in charge of your life. Have hope—look forward to Heaven; get excited about the future that I have for you. Finally, love people. I can't say it enough. It's the main point of the whole Bible. It's why I created the entire world. First, let Me love you; let My love change you. Then share My love with other people. People are an eternal investment. Love is never a waste of time, because love lasts.

The Eternal,
God

Share God's Love

Homesick
Alien Blues

LOGON>>

<TEEN> God, sometimes this world is not so great.

<GOD> I agree. What in particular?

<TEEN> There are always bullies at school. There is violence on the news and in my city. Sometimes everything seems out of control. I feel like I don't belong.

<GOD> I understand. Would it help if I told U that UR actually an alien?

<TEEN> What???

<GOD> Yep. This planet is not your home.

This world is not our home;
we are looking forward to
our everlasting home in heaven.
h e b r e w s . 1 3 : 1 4 . t l b

If you expect the world to be like a four-star hotel with complimentary room service, a huge swimming pool, and free parking, you are going to be disappointed. Instead, think about the world as a summer school, and it will make more sense. Sure it's hot, the lessons are tough, and sometimes you have to sit next to people with bad breath. But you also get to go on field trips, learn a lot, and get prepared for next year. And don't forget the best thing about summer school—it doesn't last forever.

There are some very beautiful things in the world that were created by My hand—forests, mountains, and beautiful, kind people. But there are also some very ugly things in the world that I had nothing to do with—prejudice, hatred, abuse, violence, greed, and injustice. This is the reality of your world. The good news is, I am still in control of the world, and My justice will ultimately triumph. Until then, know that you were born to live forever in a far better place. This planet is not your permanent home.

Your Creator,
God

Focus On Forever

Unsolved Mysteries

LOGON>>

<TEEN> God, sometimes I don't understand U.

<GOD> My focus is usually not your focus. I see the beginning from the end.

<TEEN> Sometimes it's frustrating not knowing the answers: why, where, how . . .

<GOD> That's where trust becomes your key partner. Trust Me.

My thoughts and my ways
are higher than yours.
i s a i a h . 5 5 : 9 . c e v

There's a saying: "Perfect comprehension is not a prerequisite for obedience." In other words, you can obey Me without understanding every single thing about Me. You really only need to know a few things in order to trust me: I am God, I can do anything, I love you, I only want to bless you. It's great to be curious about Me and ask questions, but don't get frustrated if you don't understand everything all at once.

I'm an infinite God, and you are a finite being. So sometimes My plans will seem strange to you. But if you trust Me, then you'll follow Me. I know where we're going, and I know the best road to take to get there.

Your Loving Father,
God

God Has the Map

Family Business

LOGON >>

<TEEN> Jesus, when U were growing up, how did U get to know about the Father? Were U born knowing everything?

<JESUS> Not at all. I was born as a normal human baby, drooling and crying and burping and nursing. I learned the normal way—by reading, studying, praying, observing, asking questions.

<TEEN> Who did U ask?

<JESUS> My parents, priests, teachers, anybody who was supposed to know anything about God, and I also asked God himself.

I must be about my Father's business.

luke.2:49.nkjv

When I was a kid, My parents accidentally left Me in Jerusalem. This would be like if your family took a trip to the biggest city you know, and your parents drove off without you. But I wasn't scared or afraid. I stayed behind to be in church. When My parents came back to look for Me, they found Me in church talking to the leaders, asking them questions about My Heavenly Father. It just seemed like the normal thing for Me to do. I didn't mean to disrespect My parents; I was just trying to learn more about God.

It's normal for kids to learn about their parents' jobs. If your father works at a factory, you will probably hear all about it. If your father is a mechanic, you will grow up around tools and engines and learn about cars. But you have a Heavenly Father too, and He wants you to learn about His business as well. His business is caring for the hurting people of the world. His business is being friends with the losers. He works for justice and mercy. Reading the Bible and asking questions of other Christians is a good place to start.

Your Brother,
Jesus

Learn God's Business

Team Jesus

LOGON>>

<TEEN> Jesus, I think I am one of Your disciples.

  <JESUS> Do U follow me? R U learning from Me?

  <TEEN> Yes.

    <JESUS> Then UR indeed one of My disciples. U represent Me, and I'm proud to have U on My team.

*God has given us
the privilege of urging
everyone to come into his favor
and be reconciled to him.*
2corinthians.5:18.tlb

If you're a professional guitarist, guitar companies will actually pay you to use their guitars. They'll give you free guitars and free strings and all you have to do is tell people that you play their guitars. The same goes for professional athletes. If you're a good enough tennis player, you get free rackets and a bunch of money just to use them. For example, Michael Jordan is sponsored by Nike, and in return Michael Jordan endorses Nike products.

Now get this, I'm sponsoring you to tell people about Me, to endorse Me, to encourage people to get to know Me and follow Me. This is not your job, it's your privilege. I'm proud of you. I want you to represent Me. I believe when you endorse Me, people are going to listen up. I'm offering you a wonderful life. Wear your faith in Me with pride.

Your Sponsor,
Jesus

Represent God

They Don't Need a Cure. They Need a Final Solution.

LOGON>>

<TEEN> Jesus, isn't being nice to people enough? Do I really have to tell them about U?

<JESUS> Ha! If someone has a splitting headache, giving them a cold rag is not enough. U want to give them some aspirin. Kindness is the cold rag. My salvation is the aspirin.

<TEEN> But what if they don't choose U? What if they think I'm some sort of religious freak?

<JESUS> You're not responsible for how people respond to Me. You're only responsible to tell them about Me. The rest is up to Me.

Jesus is the only One who can save people.

acts.4:12.ncv

There are a thousand different religions, schemes, plans, and offers that promise a better life. You hear it on the TV all the time, "Satisfaction guaranteed, or your money back!" But no other religion, plan, or program can save people from their sin. I am the only hope. I am the only one powerful enough to rescue people from their rebellion against God. I am the only one who can deliver them from their pain and brokenness.

When you meet people who are hurting, you can give them good advice, be nice to them, and tell them everything's going to be OK, but your first priority is to lead them to Me. You know Me, the only one able to save. I am the final solution.

The Only Savior,
Jesus

Lead Others to God

Recharge

LOGON>>

<TEEN> Father, how regularly should I have a prayer time?
How often should I read the Bible? Once a week? Once a month?

<GOD> Every day.

<TEEN> Wow. I need to recharge that much?

<GOD> It's like a spiritual battery. Time with Me charges
your spirit.

It's crucial that we keep a firm grip
on what we've heard so
that we don't drift off.
hebrews.2:1.msg

Following Me is kind of like being a long-distance runner. To be a professional distance runner, you have to stay in shape. Even if you are in top physical shape today, all it takes is a month of not running, and you begin to get out of shape. So it's not enough just to get to the top of your game; you have to stay there.

The same is true with the Christian life. You can be riding high, obeying Me, meeting with Me every day, reading your Bible, serving people, growing in every way. But all it takes is a few weeks without your regular prayer time, and temptation begins to creep in. Laziness, compromise, even doubt and fear can overtake you sooner than you think. So read the Bible regularly. Keep My words at the front of your mind and in the center of your heart. You can even choose a verse and repeat it over and over to yourself throughout the day. The devil would like to lead you off course and get you out of spiritual shape. Don't let it happen! Be diligent. Recharge every day.

Your Trainer,
God

LOGON>>

<TEEN> Father, should I become a missionary?

<GOD> U already R a missionary to the people around U.

<TEEN> Should I go to another country to tell people about U?

<GOD> If U want to touch nations, the best place to start is in prayer.

From one person God made all nations who live on earth, and he decided when and where every nation would be. God has done all this, so that we will look for him and reach out and find him.

acts.17:26-27.cev

Christianity is not just a Western religion. It actually started in the Middle East, right in the middle of the Western and Eastern worlds. There are Christians all over the world, even in countries where Christianity is illegal. And I care for every country in the world, for every culture in the world, and for every people group in the world. I made Adam and Eve, and all people descended from them. Everyone on the planet is part of the same race—the human race. When I look at people, I don't see colors or nationalities. I see people I created, people who need Me.

So what can you do about all the people in the world who still don't know Me? Begin to pray. The Bible says, "Ask of me, and I will make the nations your inheritance" (Psalm 2:8 NIV). Ask Me to give you My heart for a nation other than your own. Then learn about it and begin praying for the people of that nation. If you are willing, I may even send you as a missionary to that nation. Act locally and pray globally.

Ruler of Nations,
God

Pray Globally

Built For Speed

LOGON>>

<TEEN> I want to move forward with U, but my old life is holding me back.

   <GOD> I see that. It's obvious that U can't live in both worlds. U can't have it both ways.

   <TEEN> So what should I do?

   <GOD> I know it's hard, but you're going to have to make a decision. You're going to have to leave your old life behind if U want to experience all the good things I have for U.

Let us strip off every weight
that slows us down,
especially the sin that
so easily hinders our progress.
And let us run with endurance
the race that God has set before us.
h e b r e w s . 1 2 : 1 . n l t

You wouldn't put on a big winter coat, boots, and a pair of mittens to swim in a swim meet. No matter how much you trained, how strong you were, or how fast you were swimming, they would slow you down. The clothes would fill with water, and drag you down. No, you'd take all that stuff off and swim in your swimming suit. Clean, simple, aerodynamic, and light.

Your old life held sinful habits that are much like that heavy winter coat in the swimming race. So, strip off the bad habits. Leave them behind. You don't need them. They are not suitable for the race you are running. My love is all you need.

Your Goal,
God

Streamline Your Life

Realistic Optimism

LOGON>>

<TEEN> Jesus, what's the deal with the world? R U winning or losing? Is it getting better or worse?

<JESUS> What do U see?

<TEEN> Well, when I watch the news, I see things getting worse.

<JESUS> Look deeper. I am winning in ways that never make the news.

The darkness is passing and
the true light is already shining.

1john.2:8.niv

<<DOWNLOAD

I want you to have hope. I'm a God of light and hope. You already know how the history of the world ends—it ends with us hanging out in Heaven forever celebrating and enjoying each other. The good guys win!

Even now, I am winning in the world. Although there is darkness all around, My light is shining brighter and brighter. Lives are being changed; people are being healed and restored. Things are improving. There is no situation too difficult for Me. There is no darkness so dark that My light can't break through. Hope. Believe.

The Light of the World,
Jesus

Miracles-R-Us

LOGON>>

<TEEN> What do I do when I'm tempted to doubt?

<GOD> When U build your faith bigger, doubt becomes smaller.

<TEEN> Cool.

<GOD> Look at history and the miracles I've performed in the lives of people. It will give U faith for your life in the present.

I will remember the deeds of the LORD;

yes, I will remember your miracles of long ago.

p s a l m . 7 7 : 1 1 . n i v

When you're tempted to doubt, it helps to remember all the amazing things I've done in the past. Check out the Bible. Here are just a few of My miracles: I destroyed the world in a big flood, but I saved Noah and his family because Noah obeyed Me. I caused Sarah to have a son when she was ninety years old. I delivered Moses and all the Jews out of slavery in Egypt by parting the Red Sea and leading them through it on dry land. I destroyed the Egyptian army that was chasing them; I drowned them all in the Red Sea. I fed the Jews in the desert for forty years with miraculous bread from heaven. That whole time, their clothes and shoes never wore out.

I brought down the walls of Jericho with a mere shout. I helped Joshua defeat every single one of his enemies in Canaan. His friend Caleb even defeated an army of giants. Speaking of giants, I helped a teenager named David kill a huge giant named Goliath. David took him down with a slingshot! My servant Daniel got locked in a cave full of lions overnight, but the lions never touched him. I shut their mouths. This is just a small sample of My miracles. Now remember the amazing times that I've been there for you. Build your faith!

Your Power,
God

Build Your Faith

The Truth—
the Whole Truth

LOGON>>

<TEEN> Jesus, how can I make people believe that UR real?

<JESUS> U can't.

<TEEN> What?!? Then how is NE1 ever going to believe in U? How will they know to follow U?

<JESUS> The Holy Spirit convinces people of Me. He's the only one who can help them believe.

<TEEN> Then what's my job? Aren't I supposed to "witness" for U?

<JESUS> All U have to do is tell the truth about what U know.

You will be my witnesses.
acts.1:8.niv

<<DOWNLOAD

A witness is simply someone who "witnessed" something. In court, the judge says, "Call the next witness," and somebody comes forward, takes the stand, and tells the truth about what he's seen. Notice, the witness is not responsible to convince the jury or win the case or get the judge to like him. The witness is simply responsible to tell the truth about what he's seen and what he knows.

You are My witness. It means you've "witnessed" Me. You know Me. You've talked to Me. You've heard from Me. You've seen Me do things in your life and in the world around you. So when you "witness" for Me, all you have to do is tell the truth about what you've seen and what you know of Me. For instance, if somebody says, "God doesn't speak to people anymore," you can say, "That's not true. God speaks to at least one person. Me. He spoke to Me this morning." Tell people what you know about Me, answer their questions honestly, and I will take care of the rest.

The Truth,
Jesus

Be a Witness

Children
of Wisdom

LOGON>>

<TEEN> Father, what's the difference between wisdom and knowledge?

<GOD> A very wise question ;-) Knowledge is just facts and right answers. Wisdom is putting the truth into practice.

<TEEN> So let me see if I've got this right. Knowledge is stuff U know, but wisdom is doing the stuff U know?

<GOD> Impressive! How did U get to be so wise? ;-)

Wisdom is the principal thing;
Therefore get wisdom.
And in all your getting, get understanding.

proverbs 4:7 nkjv

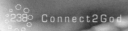

I want you to be wise. You should check out the book of Proverbs in the Bible. It's full of My wisdom. But don't just learn it; put it into practice. I want people in the world to know what true wisdom looks like. One way they'll learn is by watching My children.

As you live a wise life, people will see you and be impressed. When they ask you, "How did you know to do that? Why did that work out for you?" you can tell them about Me and My ways. Don't wait until you're old to become wise. I want to teach you My ways while you are young. I'm the wisest person in the universe, and I want to share My wisdom with you. Let Me teach you now, and others will come to know Me because of your wisdom.

Your Teacher,
God

Be Wise

Take It Personally

LOGON>>

<TEEN> Father, today some people put U down. They were talking bad about U, and it made me mad!

<GOD> All right! It should make U mad. What did U do?

<TEEN> I couldn't help myself. I didn't want to start an argument, but I had to speak up and put my two cents in. I told them U weren't like that.

<GOD> Well done! I'm proud of U!

*Zeal for your house consumes me,
and the insults of those who insult you fall on me.*

psalm.69:9.niv

King David was a big fan of mine. He really loved Me. I called him "a man after My own heart." He cared about the things I care about. So when people put Me down, he took it personally. When people put down My Church and My people, it upset him. I want you to be the same way.

When people you know make fun of Me and the values I represent, I don't want you to get into a fistfight with them, but you don't have to pretend to agree with them either. Take a stand for Me. Speak out. You don't even have to respond in anger. Just share how you feel about Me. Tell them what I mean to you. People often talk bad about Me because they don't understand what I'm like. If they say, "God doesn't care about us," tell them it's not true. Explain how I care for you. When people say, "Church is just full of a bunch of hypocrites," invite them to your church to see a different side of things. I want you to identify with Me and speak out for Me. Be passionate for Me. I'm passionate for you.

Your Fan,
God

Be Wholehearted
For God

The Best
For the Best

```
LOGON>>
```

<TEEN> Father, I want to do more for You. Sometimes it seems like there's nothing I can give You that You don't already have. What can I give You?

<GOD> You can give me your best.

<TEEN> But what does that look like practically, from day to day?

<GOD> Excellent question. It means giving me your best work, your best time, your best effort, even your best clothes. For example, if you ever have the chance to give clothes to a missionary, don't just give them ratty hand-me-downs. Give them quality clothes.

"I will not offer to the LORD my God sacrifices that have cost me nothing."

2samuel.24:24.tev

There are people who buy new paint for their house, and then they give their leftover paint to the church. I want your best. I don't want your leftovers. I want to see people paint the church with the best first, and then paint their house. It hurts My heart to see My children go through their entire day without even saying hello to Me, and then tack on a quick prayer right before they go to sleep. I want you to start your day off with Me and give Me your prime time.

One time King David wanted to build an altar to worship Me. They tried to give him the altar land for free, but David insisted on buying the land with his own money. After David died, his son King Solomon built a beautiful temple for Me on that same land. Solomon made sure he had finished building My temple before he even started working on his own house. Do you see a pattern? I want your best just as I've given you My best.

The Almighty,
God

Give God Your Best

Made by God

LOGON>>

<TEEN>   God, sometimes I feel weird, like I don't fit in.

<GOD>   Well, UR unique.

<TEEN>   But why did U make me this way? Why do I look the way I do?

<GOD>   I wanted U to look that way. I didn't make U for U. I made U for Me. And I think I did a pretty good job ;-)

You have no right to argue with your Creator.
You are merely a clay pot shaped by a potter.
The clay doesn't ask, "Why did you make me this way?"

isaiah.45:9.cev

<<DOWNLOAD

Have you ever heard the term "self-made man?" It describes a person who works very hard to make a lot of money to make a name for himself in the business world. Then he can point to his achievements and say, "I did it MY way!" But in reality, there is no such thing as a self-made man, because I made every man. Your mind, your body, your skills, and your abilities—all of them are gifts from Me.

You may not like the color of your hair, your height, or the way you look. But whenever you complain about the way I made you, you are really saying, "I don't like Your decisions. I think You did it wrong!" I know exactly what I'm doing. You are no mistake. I have a specific plan for you, something that only you can accomplish. And I made you the way you are on purpose. I don't want a bunch of people who are exactly alike. That would be boring. I love the way you are. Thank Me for the way I made you, even if it doesn't make sense. It will. I wouldn't have you any other way.

Your Maker,
God

Just Be Yourself

Nobody Loves You Like I Do

LOGON>>

<TEEN> Father, I know U love me, but it's hard to imagine.

<GOD> I love U so much that if I started to tell U how much, I would be writing for the next 200 years.

<TEEN> But why do U love me?

<GOD> Because UR My child. I love the way U look. I love the way U think. I love the things U make. I love your heart. I love everything about U.

<TEEN> That makes me feel special :)

<GOD> UR special! Don't ever doubt it. There is no one I love more than U.

To all who received him,
to those who believed in his name,
he gave the right to become
children of God.

j o h n . 1 : 1 2 . n i v

If you have asked Jesus to be in control of your life, if you believe in Him and Me, then you are My child. Jesus died on the Cross so that you could be adopted into My family. Your earthly parents love you. Still, you were made to know perfect love, and I am the only one who can love you perfectly. And I do.

If anyone picks on you, they have to answer to Me, because you are My child. I have angels assigned to watch over you and you alone. When someone hurts your feelings, it hurts My heart. When you succeed, I dance and shout with joy. I turn to Jesus and brag, "Did you see that? Yes! That's My child!" I am cheering for you up here! I watch over you night and day. Nobody loves you more than I. You are My favorite. My precious, precious child.

Your Proud Father,
God

God is Your
Biggest Fan

Praise Me

LOGON>>

<TEEN> Lord, I'm so thankful today. I know sometimes I come to U with problems or questions, but today I just want to say how great U are!

<GOD> U don't know how proud that makes Me feel!

<TEEN> Lord, it's like I can't come up with good enough words to say how great U are. Where do I start?

<GOD> Start with the Bible.

Who among the gods is like you,
O LORD? Who is like you—majestic in holiness,
awesome in glory, working wonders?

exodus.15:11.niv

I want you to praise Me. If you're thankful, if you're glad that you are My child, if you are impressed with me, then let Me know about it. If you are a poet or a songwriter, you can write your own song. But sometimes you don't know how to start. That's where the Bible can help. It's full of praise to Me, praises that My children have already written down, praises that you can use.

Start in the book of Psalms. It's 150 songs written to Me. Some of them are asking for My help, some of them are complaints. But most of them celebrate My goodness. Pick one of those psalms that expresses how you feel and read it out loud (or even shout it!). Christian music is good too. Find a Christian song that you like, turn it up, and sing it to Me with all your heart. Psalms and songs can help you to express how you feel. I hear your heart singing, I feel your love and appreciation and wor- ship, and it makes My day.

Your Proud Father,
God

Praise the Lord!

Practice
Makes Perfect

LOGON>>

   \<TEEN\> Jesus, I feel like I've learned a lot hanging out with U.

   \<JESUS\> Awesome! Now don't stop hanging out with Me. I'm alive, and I want to speak to U every day of your life.

   \<TEEN\> What do I need to know today?

   \<JESUS\> Practice. Take the things you've learned, and try them out.

Now that you know these things,
you will be blessed if you do them

john.13:17.niv

We've had some good talks. I've enjoyed hanging out with you and getting to know you as a friend. You've read My words from the Bible; you've thought about what they mean; and hopefully you know some things now that you didn't know before. But knowing is not enough. You could memorize the entire Bible and become the world champion of Bible trivia. But if you don't do the things you know, none of it will matter.

Think of it this way—I can know how to build a house, but if I never build one, then I'm not much of a carpenter. I can know where tons of pirate treasure is buried, but if I never go dig it up, then My knowledge doesn't do Me any good. I want you to cash in on what you know about Me by putting it into practice. Trust me, pray, love people, read My Word, and spend time with Me. Do the things that you know are right, and your life will be so much better because of it. And remember, you're never alone. I'm here to help you, always.

Your Brother,
Jesus

Just Do What's Right

Index

REFERENCES

About the Author

Curt Cloninger is a writer, teacher, Web designer, Internet artist, and closet Stereolab fan. He co-authored *Email from God, More Email from God,* and *Email from God for Grads.* Curt taught middle school English for four years and has been the worship leader of a generation-X type Vineyard church for six years. He is also the author of *Fresh Styles for Web Designers* (New Riders), an industry standard book on web-specific design approaches. Curt currently teaches Multimedia Arts and Sciences at the University of North Carolina at Asheville, from whence he broadcasts his pirate signal (lab404.com) in order to facilitate a more lively remote dialogue with the Sundry Essences of Wonder.

Additional copies of this and other
Honor Books products are available
from your local bookseller.

Other great books by Curt Cloninger:

Email from God for Teens

More Email from God for Teens

Email from God for Grads

If you have enjoyed this book,
or if it has had an impact on your life,
we would like to hear from you.

Please contact us at:

Honor Books, Dept. 201
4050 Lee Vance View
Colorado Springs, CO 80918
Or visit our Web site:
www.cookministries.com

HONOR **H** BOOKS

Inspiration and Motivation for the Season of Life